D1738811

Cold Water Diving

A Guide to Ice Diving

A BEST PUBLICATION

Cold Water Diving

A Guide to Ice Diving

By John N. Heine

A BEST PUBLICATION

Copyright © 1996 by Best Publishing Company

All rights reserved

No part of this book may be reproduced, stored in a retrieval system, or trans-
mitted in any form or by any means, electronic, mechanical, photocopying,
microfilming, recording, or otherwise, without written permission from
the publisher.

ISBN: 0-941332-52-7
Library of Congress catalog card number: 95-080959

Composed, printed and bound in the United States of America.

Best Publishing Company
2355 North Steves Boulevard
P.O. Box 30100
Flagstaff, Arizona 86003-0100 USA

Table of Contents

WARNING

Scuba diving is a potentially hazardous activity. Ice diving is a special type of scuba diving which requires special equipment and training. This book is not a substitute for scuba diving or ice diving instruction. You must be certified for scuba diving, and for diving in cold water and under ice.

About the Author

John Heine is an experienced scientific and sport diver. He has dived in many areas of the world, including both poles and tropical areas in between.

John became certified as a NAUI Instructor in 1980, and as an Instructor Trainer in 1982. He is certified as an Ice Diving Specialty Instructor. He has conducted many leadership level training programs for NAUI, and was awarded NAUI's Outstanding Service Award in 1992.

He earned a B.S. in Biological Sciences from the University of California at Irvine, and a Masters Degree in Marine Science from the Moss Landing Marine Laboratories of the California State University. He is the President of the American Academy of Underwater Sciences (AAUS).

John has conducted many scientific and sport dives under the ice. He spent three seasons in Antarctica doing research dives through ice that was ten feet thick, in water temperatures of 28.6 °F (-1.9 °C), and air temperatures as low as -60 °F (-50 °C). He has also done cold water and ice diving in Alaska and in lakes in the Rocky Mountains. He serves as a member of the diving control board for the National Science Foundation, Office of Polar Programs.

John is an accomplished writer and photographer. He has published scientific articles in journals such as the *Journal of Phycology, Journal of Experimental Marine Biology and Ecology, Marine Ecology Progress Series, Polar Biology, and Journal of Chemical Ecology*. His diving-related publications include books on *Advanced Diving Technology and Techniques, and Dry Suit Diving* for NAUI, *Blue Water Diving Guidelines* for the California Sea Grant Program, and articles in the *Proceedings of the American Academy of Underwater Sciences, NOAA Diving Manual, SOURCES, the Journal of Underwater Education, and Underwater USA*. His underwater photographs have appeared in catalogs, textbooks, magazines, and educational programs. He is a contributing Editor for *SOURCES*.

John works as the Diving Safety Officer for Moss Landing Marine Laboratories of the California State University. He was also recently elected as a Commissioner of the Moss Landing Harbor District.

Acknowledgements

This publication would not have been possible without the help of many people. Thanks go to Dr. Jim McClintock for getting me to Antarctica three times to dive in some of the most spectacular under-ice areas of the world. Other members of our science party that I spent time with underwater include Marc Slattery, Jim Weston, Bill Baker, Pat Bryan and Mark Hamann. Special thanks to the National Science Foundation, Office of Polar Programs, and Antarctic Support Associates, for providing excellent support of science and scientific diving in the Antarctic. Specifically, Jim Stewart, Jim Mastro, and Jeff Bozanic were instrumental in conducting a safe scientific diving program during my years at McMurdo Station in Antarctica.

I spent many enjoyable hours with Dr. John Oliver and the Benthic Bubs of the Moss Landing Marine Laboratories, diving in the Bering and Chukchi Seas near Alaska. That was my first real introduction to cold water diving. Bill Briggs and John Brooks of the National Park Service were extremely helpful during an ice diving training course that they sponsored and I conducted.

Special thanks go to my good friend, Steve Barsky, who I have worked with on many projects. I especially thank the people who have contributed photographs and technical information for this book: Dale Andersen, Dan Bockus, John Brooks, Paul Dayton, Art DeVries, Ken Dunton, Neal Langerman, Jim Mastro, Jim McClintock, Peter Neushul, John Nickel, Terry Rioux, and Marc Slattery.

I appreciate the assistance of Neal Langerman and Dale Andersen, who critiqued early drafts of the manuscript. Joan Parker, librarian at the Moss Landing Marine Laboratories, found many obscure references for me, and Lynn McMasters assisted with the graphics.

Lastly, I thank my wife, Ann, who is extremely tolerant and supportive of my projects, which often require considerable time away from home. I also want to thank the faculty and staff at the Moss Landing Marine Laboratories, and university life in general, both of which condone and support projects like these which add to our knowledge and safety while in and under the water.

Chapter 1

An Introduction
to Ice Diving

Cold water and ice diving can be extremely challenging, yet rewarding experiences for the adventurous diver. Diving in these environments requires thoughtful planning, preparation, training, and the utmost dedication to safety. The rewards are many, including excellent visibility, having a calm surface platform to work from, the sense of accomplishment by performing an extreme challenge, and the enjoyment of being outdoors in cold weather.

Cold Water Diving

Cold water diving is defined as diving that takes place in water that is below about 40 °F (4.5 °C). Many lakes and ocean regions have water temperatures this low in seasons other than winter. While this is obviously not freezing water, it is sufficiently cold to require special thermal protection and regulator care. Hypothermia and equipment malfunction are special risks associated with cold water diving. Considerations for low surface temperatures, thermal stress, equipment malfunction, and logistics increase the complexity of this special type of diving.

Diving under ice is a special situation which increases the dive complexity, with the presence of a ceiling overhead for divers. This requires a team of surface tenders and special procedures to ensure that divers are able to return to the entry hole, as well as deal with any emergencies which might arise.

There are many things to consider when planning and executing a cold water dive. Training, equipment considerations, shelter, safety and emergency equipment, and personnel are all important. It takes considerable time to select and prepare a site, suit in and out of dry suits, and conduct the dive. The following chapters will cover these topics in detail.

History of Ice Diving

Ice diving traditionally has been limited by thermal protection, chiefly in exposure suit technology. In the early 1900's, salvage divers in Iceland were stationed on board vessels to render assistance to fishing boats whose nets became entangled. They used relatively crude commercial diving dress. With the advent of scuba equipment in the 1950's, the Icelandic Coast Guard began training personnel for open sea diving operations, often in water temperatures that were near freezing.

In Antarctica, scientists began diving in ice-cold water for research in 1957. Initial test dives were made to determine the feasibility of using diving equipment in these harsh environmental conditions. Wet suits, "dry" suits, and double hose regulators were utilized, and dives were made for up to a one hour duration.

Fig. 1.1 –
*A well orga-
nized ice diving
operation
requires consid-
erable planning
and preparation
(photo by Ken
Dunton)*

Fig. 1.2 –*Ice diving requires a surface support team for the divers (photo by John Brooks)*

Custom-tailored wet suits up to 3/8 inch (9 mm) thick reportedly worked well, especially if the diver kept swimming to generate body heat. During these early southern polar dives, the first observations of the abrasive action of ice in shallow subtidal areas was documented.

The first under-ice dives were conducted in Antarctica in the early 1960's. Diving was even done in the dark months of the Antarctic winter using underwater flood lights. Divers were tethered for safety and communications reasons. Divers wore wet suits underneath dry suits with built-in mittens. While this combination proved extremely bulky, it allowed divers to remain under the ice for periods up to one hour.

In the mid-1950's, Canadian naval divers began arctic diving operations for surveys. Research diving in cold marine and freshwater began in the 1960's. In the Sub-Igloo expedition, an 8 foot (2.5 m) transparent sphere was anchored to the sea floor in the Canadian Arctic to support divers underwater. It was found that human efficiency underwater could be enhanced by the presence of a rest station offering air and warmth.

Fig. 1.3 –
*Early ice divers
wore wet suits
and used double
hose regulators
(photo by Dale
Andersen)*

More recently, ice diving has been associated with oil and gas development and mining activities. In the Arctic, a "controlled" oil spill experiment found that under the ice oil seeps up towards the surface of the ice through small hollow brine channels, which then freeze, essentially sandwiching the oil into the ice.

Naval oceanographers conducted early under-ice scuba dives in the Arctic region near Point Barrow, Alaska, to evaluate equipment, safety, and efficiency of dives in harsh, freezing conditions. They used two stage double hose primary regulators, and various types of single hose regulators as backups, wet suits, and the first commercial dry suit, the Poseidon Unisuit.

The JIM suit, which is a commercial diving one atmosphere diving suit, was used in the Arctic on dives to 905 feet (272 m), where the water temperature was 27.5 °F (-3 °C). The suit is heated by the diver's body heat and CO_2 scrubbers, which stabilize the system at 70 °F (21 °C). This allowed an underwater time of 5 hours and 59 minutes on the dive.

The Cold Water and Ice Diving Environment

Seasonal Thermal Stratification in Lakes

Lakes in the temperate zone have a general seasonal pattern of thermal stratification. During the summer months the upper two meters of lake water will absorb more than one-half of the sun's radiation and will be warmed. A typical summer stratification has three distinct water layers. The epilimnion is the surface layer of warm water, typically 55 °F (13 °C) to 75 °F (24 °C) , which reaches down to a depth of about 30-50 feet (10-15m). Below this layer is a region of sharp decline in temperature, termed the thermocline or metalimnion. The temperature here can drop by as much as 30 °F (15 °C) in just a few meters of depth. The lowest layer of water is called the hypolimnion, which is a deep, cold, undisturbed layer

Fig. 1.4 –
Dry suit and double hose regulator used in the Antarctic, 1962 (photo by Art DeVries)

Fig. 1.5 –*One of the first dry suits to be used for ice diving was the Poseidon Unisuit*

Fig. 1.6 –*Pioneering scientific divers wore prototype dry suits in the Antarctic in the 1950's (photo courtesy Peter Neushul)*

of water which approaches the temperature of maximum density for fresh water, 39 °F (4 °C).

In the fall, as air temperatures begin to cool, and the sun is not as high in the sky, the water cools to about 43 °F (6 °C) and wind-induced mixing of the water layers begins. This so-called Fall turnover results in an isothermal condition where the water temperature is about 39 °F (4 °C) from the surface to the bottom.

As winter ensues, further cooling of surface water occurs, and ice begins to form. A reverse stratification can occur, where colder (less dense) water overlies warmer (more dense) water.

In the spring, as ice melts and day length increases, the wind can induce a spring turnover which produces relatively isothermal water conditions of around 39 °F(4 °C). This is a general description of stratification in large temperate lakes, and many variations will be found due to climate, lake morphology, and movement of water masses.

Fig. 1.7 –*Early scientific divers in Antarctica used wet suits, twin cylinders, and double hose regulators (photo by Paul Dayton)*

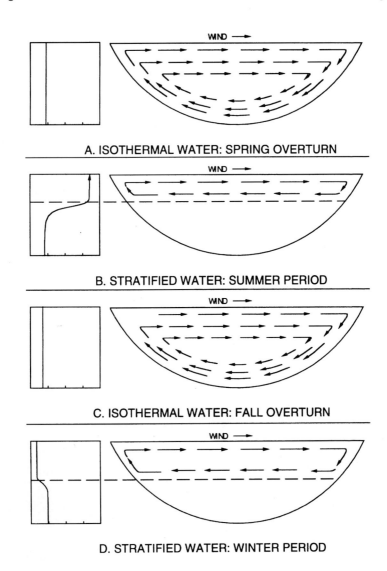

A. ISOTHERMAL WATER: SPRING OVERTURN

B. STRATIFIED WATER: SUMMER PERIOD

C. ISOTHERMAL WATER: FALL OVERTURN

D. STRATIFIED WATER: WINTER PERIOD

Fig. 1.8a –*Four seasons of lake stratification*

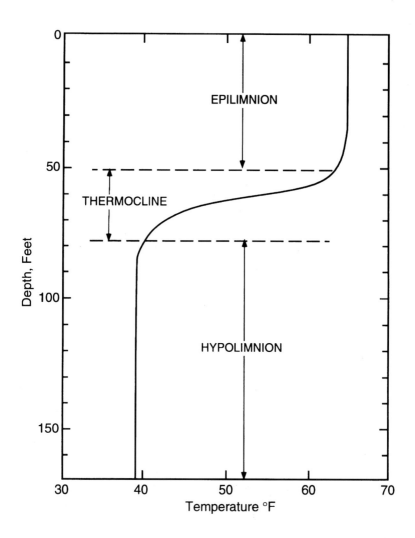

Fig. 1.8b –*Lake water layer terminology*

Variation in Ocean Temperatures

Ocean surface layer temperatures can be extremely variable, depending upon such factors as latitude, climate, winds, and ocean currents. An example is shown from an open ocean station off the coast of Siberia. In March the water is at a uniform temperature of about 40 °F (4.5 °C). The water continues to warm through the summer, and a marked thermocline develops, the depth of which is dependent upon wind conditions. A typical maximum temperature of 60 °F (15.5 °C) is reached. In the fall, as the surface water cools, it becomes denser and sinks. Winter conditions show uniform cold temperatures down to depths of 225 feet (70m).

Other areas may show variations in ocean temperature that are related more to currents and wind patterns, rather than large changes in air temperature or available sunlight. In California, the prevailing current runs from north to south, bringing colder water along the coastline. Interestingly, the warmest water can be present in the winter, when the current typically runs south to north. In the springtime, strong northwesterly winds cause upwelling, where surface waters are blown away from shore and are replaced by deeper, cold water.

On the east coast of the United States, the Gulf Stream runs from south to north, bathing the coastline in relatively warm water. Northern states and eastern Canada undergo winter freezing of the ocean waters due to the cold Labrador current flowing from the north.

In the Arctic regions, new ice forms in the winter and melts during the following summer. In the Antarctic, the seasons are reversed. Although highly variable depending on the latitude and weather, new ice generally forms in the austral fall and winter (March-November) and melts in the austral summer (December-February).

Ice diving can be conducted in both fresh and salt water. The characteristics of ice are different for these two media, and are discussed below. It is important for divers to have some knowledge of the physics behind ice formation, strength, and types of ice.

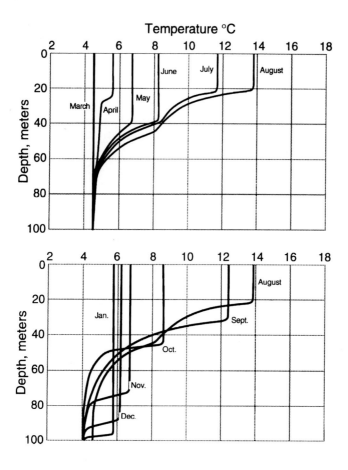

Fig. 1.9 –*An example of the seasonal variation of ocean temperature in the North Pacific.*

Fresh Water Ice

Most liquids expand somewhat uniformly with increasing temperature. However, fresh water has a somewhat different pattern than other liquids. Between around 32-39 °F (0-4 °C), water contracts as the temperature increases. At 39°F (4 °C), water has the least volume and maximum density. Pure water expands about

Fig. 1.10 –*New ice is formed in sheets that are broken up by the wind and waves (photo by Dan Bockus)*

9% on freezing. This is the reason why ice floats and lakes freeze from the surface down!

Cold air temperatures cause the surface water to cool, and when the water reaches 39 °F (4 °C) it becomes denser and sinks. This displaces warmer water up to the surface, which then becomes chilled. This continual mixing occurs, and the bottom water stays at a temperature of around 39 °F (4 °C), while the colder, less dense surface water freezes.

In North America most alpine lakes and rivers north of about 35 °N usually have some ice cover each winter. Some large lakes, such as some of the Great Lakes, never form a complete ice cover due to strong winds blowing over a relatively deep body of water. This causes an upwelling of slightly warmer water to the surface, which delays the onset of freezing. However, a significant portion of the Great Lakes is covered with anywhere from 2 to 16 inches of ice during the winter. Underwater visibility under this ice can be as great as 100 feet in Lake Superior, and remarkably lower in areas where there is significant run-off, nutrient enrichment, and fine sediment.

Some terms used to describe fresh water ice are clear ice, which is nearly transparent, bubbly ice, which is translucent due to the trapped air bubbles, and snow ice, which is opaque or milky in appearance.

Lake Environments

Lakes vary tremendously with respect to water visibility, bottom terrain, thermoclines, and potential hazards. Many mountain lakes are clear, while lower-lying reservoirs or glacial lakes may be cloudy. The bottom terrain can consist of soft fine sediments which can be easily disturbed, to rocky ledges of varying slopes.

There are potential hazards in some lakes and quarries which may impede a dive. In areas around dams or near roads there may be old cables, heavy equipment, fishing line, hooks, lures, and even automobiles. There is also a possibility of encountering tree limbs, or submerged structures.

If the lake is at altitude, the appropriate altitude tables, conversions, or dive computers must be utilized.

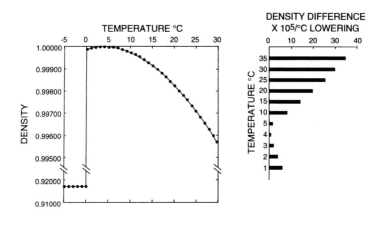

Fig. 1.11 —*Fresh water has a unique pattern of density at different temperatures*

Rivers

Diving in cold or frozen rivers can be dangerous. No dive should be conducted under a frozen river where a current exists, as divers can be swept into areas where it is impossible to surface. Potential hazards underwater include tree limbs, sharp rocks, fishing line, hooks, lures, and nets.

Sea Ice

The low air temperature conditions of high latitude regions can cause the freezing of sea water. Normal salinity of seawater is 35 parts per thousand. This seawater will freeze at a temperature of 28.6 °F (-1.9 °C). As the water cools, small crystals called frazil, begin to form. The dissolved solids are excluded from the frozen crystals, so that sea ice has a much lower salinity than the surrounding water. A slushy mixture develops, which is called grease ice, which will form into a thin frozen sheet if conditions are calm. Wind and wave action can break these thin sheets into what is called pancake ice, which are small disks of ice about 1-3 feet

Fig. 1.12 –*Many alpine lakes freeze over during the winter*

Fig. 1.13 –
*Diver observing
a crustacean in a
mountain lake
(photo by John
Brooks)*

(0.3-1m) in diameter. With further freezing, these disks can join together to form floes. Freezing generally continues from the bottom of the ice.

There are a number of various types of sea ice. Pack ice forms seasonally in polar regions, moves with the wind and currents, and can be up to 6.5 feet (2m) thick. It can be semi-permanent above 75° latitude. When this ice collides together, breaks up, and melts and refreezes, the pack ice can take on a rough and jagged appearance. This is sometimes called multi-year ice, because of its age, and can be up to 12-20 feet (4-6 m) thick. Polar ice, which is permanent ice, can be in excess of 165 feet (50m) thick. Fast ice is solid ice which is connected to the shoreline. It develops in the winter, and disappears in summer, and is usually about 6 feet (2m) thick. This ice sheet continues to grow from the underside by the freezing of platelet ice crystals. These types of sea ice rarely exceed 13 feet (4m) in thickness.

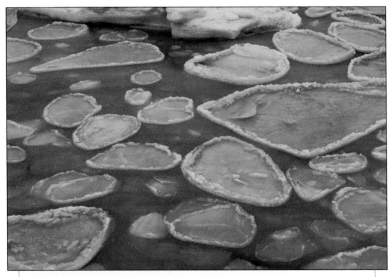

Fig. 1.14 –*Pancake ice (photo by Jim Mastro)*

Fig. 1.15 –*Sea ice sheets break up and move with the wind and current, and is called pack ice (photo by Terry Rioux)*

Fig. 1.16 –*Larger ice floes can be dangerous for divers below*

Fig. 1.17 –*Fast ice is frozen to the shoreline*

Fig. 1.18 –
*Brine channels
are underwater
pinnacles which
concentrate salt
in sea ice*

The small amount of salt in sea ice is concentrated in pockets of brine, forming brine channels, which are like underwater pinnacles hanging below the ice surface.

Chapter 2

Training

Ice diving can be a demanding and highly technical endeavor. It is difficult to state a set of prerequisites for entry into ice diving training, as it can vary widely between people, but certainly the diver must be very comfortable in the water. It is suggested that as a minimum the diver be certified as an advanced diver, have at least 50 logged open water dives, and have prior dry suit training in open water.

Students in training should be expected to provide the usual openwater diving equipment, which additionally should include a dry suit, a scuba cylinder with dual regulator valve (or a separate pony cylinder with regulator), two single-hose regulators appropriate for the water temperature, and a safety harness. The instructor may provide some of the equipment above, in addition to down-lines with flashers, safety lines, clips, ice cutting equipment, ice screws, emergency equipment, and shelter.

Classroom Curriculum

A sample outline of topics to be discussed in the classroom is provided. The length of classroom presentations will be dictated by the level of training required.

A. Cold Weather Environment

Climate and weather
Temperature extremes
Orientation to local conditions
Windchill
Frostbite
Hypothermia
Sunburn, snowblindness

Fig. 2.1– *Formal ice diving training is absolutely necessary for anyone wishing to dive under the ice*

B. Cold Water Environment

Physics of water
Fresh and salt water ice formation
Types of ice
Seasonal stratification in lakes
Orientation to local conditions

C. Equipment

Thermal protection: dry suits and undergarments
Accessories: hoods, gloves, mitts, mask, fins, knife
Weight and buoyancy systems
Cylinders and valves
Regulators
Lights, gauges, batteries
Safety harness and tether lines, caribiners
Tender equipment: layering for warmth and flexibility;
    boots, gloves

Emergency equipment: First aid, oxygen, warm blankets,
   hot water, communications
Hole cutting equipment: chain saws, ice screws, shovels
Shelter, heating

D. Ice Diving Operations

Evaluating ice conditions
Preparing the dive site
Cutting and clearing the dive hole
Erecting a shelter

E. Dive Planning and Personnel

Obtaining a weather forecast
Tenders duties and responsibilities
Safety diver responsibilities
Dive plan review
Line pull signals
Altitude diving considerations

Fig. 2.2 –*The ice diving instructor will normally provide equipment such as a hole drilling auger, (photo by Ken Dunton)*

F. The Dive

Suiting up
Entry techniques
Descent
Buoyancy control
Air management
Communications with surface personnel
Exit

G. Safety and Emergency Procedures

Environmental hazards: currents, wind, visibility, cold
Entanglement
Regulator freeze-up

Fig. 2.3 –
*and chain saw
(photo by Ken
Dunton)*

Fig. 2.4 – *Photographs depicting actual ice diving are very useful for classroom presentations*

Inflator valve malfunction
Dropped or lost weight belt
Flooded dry suit
Loss of dive hole
Locating a lost diver; deploying the safety diver
Diver rescue
First aid, oxygen administration
Emergency evacuation

Confined Water Training

Confined water (pool) training is considered to be optional by many ice diving instructors. It is beneficial, however, if the instructor is not familiar with the students skills in dry suit techniques, regulator recovery and switching, and buoyancy control.

If required, confined water sessions should be conducted to familiarize participants with dry suit use including problem solving, entries and exits, switching over from a freezing regulator,

Fig. 2.5 – *Confined water training is helpful to practice techniques to be used in actual ice dives*

line pull communications with the tender, and lost diver/lost exit hole procedures. Pool covers can be used to simulate the overhead environment provided by ice.

Dry Suit Training

Dry suits are complex pieces of diving equipment and require training to become familiar and comfortable with their use. You should complete a thorough dry suit training course before attempting to use a dry suit. While dry suits are not particularly difficult to use, there are a number of special procedures you should learn from a qualified instructor.

Divers accustomed to wearing wet suits may find a dry suit to be uncomfortable and cumbersome at first. This is due to a number of reasons. The first is the fact that dry suits generally consist of two layers: an outer waterproof shell which covers an inner layer of undergarments. They can be somewhat bulky out of water. Secondly, in order to be waterproof, there are seals at the neck and wrists which must fit snugly against the skin in order to keep the water out of the suit. You will become more used to these seals with time.

Ice Diving "Open Water" Water Training

A minimum of three ice dives should be conducted in initial training. The first ice dive will be spent with a thorough orientation and preparation of the site. Dive holes must be cut, shelters erected, and emergency equipment staged. Trainees should rotate with surface tenders and personnel so that everyone gets a chance to act in all roles. The dive will consist of a limited (i.e. 50 ft/15 m) horizontal distance from the entry hole, with a maximum of two trainees per instructor. This is essentially a familiarization dive so that the trainees understand the complexity and time involved with conducting an ice dive. Line pull signals with the tenders are to be practiced.

The subsequent dives will stress line signals, buoyancy control, problem solving, and emergency procedures drills. Specific scenar-

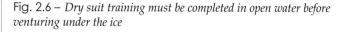

Fig. 2.6 – *Dry suit training must be completed in open water before venturing under the ice*

Fig. 2.7 –
*There are special
procedures for
using a dry suit
under the ice
(photo by Jim
McClintock)*

ios can be constructed and played out by the trainees under the supervision of the instructional staff. Careful practice of simulated suit blow-up, lost or dropped weight belt, simulated lost diver procedures, simulated regulator malfunction, and rescues can be conducted. The post dive debriefing is a key part of all dive training.

All participants should rotate through the various support and diver positions, so that they have some training and appreciation for the responsibilities involved. Students should not be allowed to actually be responsible for tending, but can assist under supervision. The instructor will of course be in a position to supervise and evaluate the ice diving training. This might include both surface and underwater supervision, so the presence of appropriate trained assistants is essential.

Fig. 2.8 –
*Training
includes close
observation of
divers by an
Instructor
(photo by John
Brooks)*

Fig. 2.9 –
*A last brief
review of the
dive plan
between tender
and diver*

Fig. 2.10 – *The initial ice dive consists of a limited horizontal swim under the close supervision of the instructor*

Fig. 2.11 – *Buoyancy control and trim are important skills to be learned for ice diving (photo by Jim Mastro)*

Fig. 2.12 – *Advanced ice diving training might include the use of full face masks,*

Fig. 2.13 – *or diving helmets with hard wire verbal communications (photo by Ken Dunton)*

Chapter 3

Equipment for
Ice Diving

Diving is an equipment intensive activity. Ice diving requires an extensive amount of additional equipment because of the cold weather and water, remote locations involved, and the presence of an overhead obstruction during the dive. It is important for ice divers to understand the requirements and options for equipment, in order to make informed purchases and decisions.

Thermal Protection for Divers

Diving is no fun if you are cold. It can also be hazardous if a diver gets hypothermia. Divers in cold water have a higher air consumption rate, expend more energy, and can become more fatigued than divers in warmer water. Cold water also decreases a diver's ability to perform complex tasks that require manual dexterity. Dry suits offer benefits such as increasing the warmth and comfort of the diver, they help conserve energy which results in less fatigue, and they are warmer on the surface between dives, especially in the wind.

Neoprene wet suits can be worn on shorter, shallow ice dives, but modern dry suits are preferable. A neoprene wet suit compresses dramatically with depth, due to the air spaces in the material. This causes a significant reduction in the insulating properties of the material. Most dry suit materials do not compress with depth, and air is added to the inside of the suit to overcome the compression of the air spaces in the undergarments. This means that the insulative value of the dry suit does not change greatly with depth, as it does in a wet suit.

Dry suits require more care and maintenance than wet suits. Most of this maintenance you can do yourself. They also require some training in the proper use and care of the dry suit.

Fig. 3.1 –
*Ice diving
requires a con-
siderable
amount of
equipment
(photo by Ken
Dunton)*

Types of Dry Suits

Dry suits are made out of a number of different types of materials. There are advantages and disadvantages to each type.
The original type of dry suit material is closed cell (or foam) neoprene, the same material used to make wet suits. The benefits of
this type of material are that it has good stretch, provides considerable insulation without undergarments, and is relatively inexpensive. The disadvantages include the considerable buoyancy of
the material which requires a large amount of weight, and the fact
that this material compresses with depth, which reduces its insulation effects, and creates large changes in buoyancy.

Closed cell neoprene dry suits are constructed similar to wet
suits, using glue and stitching. The seams will deteriorate with
age, but are relatively easy to repair. The material is also subject to
punctures from barnacles, sea urchin spines, and other sharp

objects. However, the neoprene is usually covered with nylon to promote resistance to wear by abrasion. The neck and wrist seals are usually made of neoprene as well, but latex seals can be specially ordered.

Crushed neoprene dry suits use thick neoprene which has been compressed. The advantage to this is that the material is denser, which decreases its inherent buoyancy, yet makes it stronger while retaining its stretch. This type of suit fits close to the body, which decreases the drag associated with baggy suits. The seams may be glued, stitched, and/or taped. The seals can be either neoprene or latex. These suits are expensive, but will provide many years of service.

The remaining types of dry suits fall into the category of shell suits. These dry suits themselves provide no buoyancy and minimal if any insulation, but serve only to keep the diver dry. Insulation is achieved by wearing undergarments beneath the dry suit.

The first type of shell suit is made of tri-laminate material, which is composed of three layers: nylon on the inside and outside with a layer of rubber in the middle. The material is very strong,

Fig. 3.2 –*Before the advent of dry suits, wet suits were worn under the ice (photo D. Andersen)*

resistant to abrasion, and is lightweight, but does not stretch. It rolls up into a very small package, and dries very quickly, which makes it desirable for travel. Latex wrist and neck seals are usually found on tri-laminate dry suits.

A more economical material that is used in shell suits is urethane-backed nylon. It has similar properties of the tri-laminate material but is thinner, and stiffer. Since the material does not stretch, these suits often have a somewhat baggy appearance, as they must fit looser to allow entry and exit from the suit.

The final type of shell dry suit material is vulcanized rubber, which is usually made from a combination of natural and synthetic rubber. The material is bonded together under heat and pressure which produces a very strong bond. These suits have some stretch, which makes them easier to don and comfortable to wear. The material is strong, easy to patch, dries very quickly, and lasts many years. Many repairs can be made by the user at the dive site. Various thicknesses are available for the range of diving needs.

Fig. 3.3 –*The Poseidon Unisuit was one of the first foam neoprene dry suits*

Fig. 3.4 –
*The DUI CF 200
is a crushed neo-
prene dry suit*

Features of Dry Suits

All dry suits share some essential features such as a waterproof zipper, inflation and exhaust valves, and neck and wrist seals, but there are many options and styles available.

The waterproof zipper is the most critical, and expensive, part of a dry suit. It should be large and strong. The longer the zipper the more expensive it is. The length of the zipper is primarily a function of where it is placed on the suit. Dry suit zippers can be placed horizontally across the back of the shoulders, diagonally from one shoulder across the chest to the opposite hip, or from the back under the crotch, to the front.

The most common location of the zipper is along the back between the shoulders. This requires the assistance of your buddy to open and close the zipper when dressing in and out. This zipper location can restrict movement if it is not long enough,

Fig. 3.5 –
There are a variety of shell suits available that keep the diver dry

and the zipper can take some physical abuse from the buoyancy compensator rubbing against it.

The self-donning type of dry suit has a zipper that runs diagonally across the chest. The advantages to this are that the diver can completely dress in and out of the suit without assistance, as well as easily open it between dives. Care must be taken not to lay on the bottom and get sediment into the zipper. Some suits have a zipper guard, which is a layer of extra material that protects the waterproof zipper.

The last type of zipper placement runs from front to back under the crotch. This requires a very long zipper that is more expensive, and harder to maintain. Suits with this design also tend to be baggier.

Dry suit neck and wrist seals are made of either neoprene or latex rubber. Neoprene neck seals are usually 1/8 inch (3mm) thick, and the wrist seals can vary from 1/8 to 1/4 inch (3-7 mm) thick. The smooth side of the neoprene seals against the diver's skin. They can be configured to either lie flat against the skin, or to be rolled under an inch or so to seal against the skin. Neoprene should not be trimmed to make the seals larger, but should be slowly and gradually stretched. Neoprene seals are difficult to repair in the field, as the material must be totally dry before repairs can be made, and the cement requires time to cure. See the manufacturer's recommendations before repairing or altering your seals.

Latex rubber seals are thin, stretchy, and strong. They come in a variety of thicknesses. These seals can be trimmed to fit with sharp scissors, but if you are not experienced with this procedure it is best to leave this to a dealer.

New dry suit divers will often mistake a correct fitting neck seal as too tight, and may trim it back too far. It should fit snug,

Fig. 3.6 –
*Viking makes a
durable vulcan-
ized rubber
dry suit*

Fig. 3.7 –
*A self-donning
dry suit has a
front entry that
allows the user
to zip and unzip
the suit*

but not so tight as to restrict breathing and circulation. If you are in doubt, see your dealer. Latex seals are vulnerable to puncture from sharp fingernails, jewelry, and marine life. However, they are not difficult to repair in the field.

All dry suit seals are subject to wear and tear, and will need to be replaced periodically. You should have them replaced when they start to leak, or if they become torn.

Modern dry suit inflation and deflation valves allow the diver to control the volume of air in the dry suit, which affects both the buoyancy and thermal protection of the diver. The inflator valve operates similar to a BC low pressure inflator mechanism. It is usually mounted in the chest region of the suit. A quick-disconnect low pressure hose from the regulator first stage attaches to the inflator valve for power inflation. Some neoprene dry suits have a power inflator mounted onto a corrugated hose, which also allows oral inflation, and manual deflation from the same valve.

Inflator valves can freeze-up and free flow if there is moisture in the mechanism. Valves should be dry, and any snow or water should be blown dry off an inflator hose before attachment. Divers should use only brief (i.e. one second) bursts of air from the valve, and avoid depressing it for longer periods. Holding the valve open for extended periods can cause free flow. Divers should practice disconnecting the inflator hose in case of freeze-up.

The exhaust valve is usually located on the upper arm area of the dry suit. A manual exhaust valve must be operated by hand, which requires pressing on it to release air on ascent. Automatic exhaust valves can be adjusted by the diver to control the rate of exhaust from the dry suit. By setting it in the open position before ascent, the valve will automatically vent off the expanding air as the ambient pressure decreases. The valve must be at the highest point of the dry suit to allow all of the air to escape. Most of these automatic valves have a manual over-ride feature, which allows the valve to be fully opened by depressing the valve by hand.

Fig. 3.8 –
A dry suit with a back, or shoulder zipper (photo J. Brooks)

Custom sizing is available for most dry suits, but usually is not necessary. The size you will use is based on your height, weight, and shoe size. There should be enough room for the dive undergarments, and to allow bending and squatting without discomfort.

Accessories

Some of the more inexpensive dry suits have ankle seals or thin latex boots. The preferred dry suits have attached boots made of heavy duty neoprene, or molded sole rubber. Most attached boots are quite large, and require the use of fins with large foot pockets. Knee pads are also desirable, as this is often a location that is subject to considerable wear.

A hood is required if the water is cold enough to warrant wearing a dry suit. Standard neoprene wet suit hoods can be used with

Fig. 3.9 –
The diver must be careful when adjusting the seals

Fig. 3.10 – *The exhaust valve is raised to allow air to escape the dry suit (photo J. Nickel)*

some dry suits. A more preferred hood is one made especially to seal against the neck seal of the dry suit. These hoods usually have a short neck, and use skin-in neoprene around the neck, and sometimes around the face, to provide a good seal against water intrusion. There are also dry hoods made out of neoprene or latex that can be attached directly to the dry suit. The latex hood uses an insulated liner, and works well in extremely cold environments. They generally do not seal against beards, or on people with very thin faces.

Regular neoprene gloves or mitts may be used with a dry suit. Colder water dictates the use of thicker gloves. Gauntlet style gloves are a good choice to give protection around latex wrist seals. Three fingered mitts are warmer than five fingered gloves, as the surface area that can be cooled is reduced. However, dexterity is reduced with mitts as compared to gloves.

In very cold ice diving conditions, special dry gloves are available that seal against rings on the arm of the dry suit. Liners worn under the dry gloves provide insulation to the hands for warmth. To prevent glove squeeze, and to promote warmth, short pieces of surgical tubing, or cocktail straws, can be inserted under the wrist

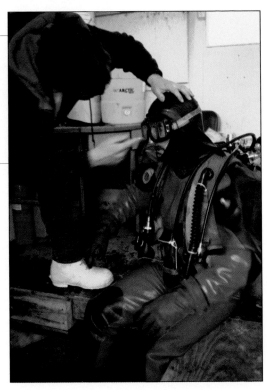

Fig. 3.11 –
*The tender
checks that the
mask is sealed
under the hood
(photo J.
McClintock)*

seals to provide a conduit for air to exchange from the suit to the gloves.

Undergarments

Dry suits are designed to keep you dry, while the undergarment's function is to keep you warm. Some thicker neoprene dry suits (1/4 inch or 7 mm) are worn without undergarments, but all shell suits require some type of insulation be worn underneath. Many types of undergarments are available, made of various material types, with different features, and prices.

The function of the undergarments is to trap air against your body to be warmed. The colder the water, the thicker or more layers of undergarments are required. Many dry suit divers wear a thin set of polypropylene liners under their thicker undergarments. This type of material helps to wick any moisture away from the body. It is also much easier to launder the thin liners than the bulkier undergarments.

Most dry suit undergarments are available in a variety of thicknesses that can be chosen depending upon the temperature of the water, the physiology of the diver, and the anticipated level of activity. Undergarments add bulk, and they must fit comfortably under the dry suit, without being too tight. The one piece "jump suit" style is the most common and comfortable configuration of dive wear. Many brands have loops at the wrist that the diver places over the thumbs when donning the dry suit. This keeps the sleeves of the undergarments from being pulled up the arm when pulling the dry suit on. The thumb loops must be tucked under the wrist seal to keep from leaking.

Fig. 3.12 –
Gloves are usually the last piece of gear to go on

The first type of undergarment is called fleece, which is also known as woolly bears, or synthetic pile. This type of material is somewhat bulky and provides good insulation on the surface. However, it compresses with depth, which decreases its insulative value. It also loses its insulation when wet. Lint from this material can clog the exhaust valve of the dry suit and cause it to leak.

The second type of undergarment is open cell foam. It offers slightly greater insulation than fleece, does not compress greatly with depth, does not produce lint, and is easy to launder. It functions when slightly damp, but will not insulate when wet.

Another type of material used in dry suit undergarments is called radiant barrier or radiant insulating material. This type of material uses an aluminum polyethylene film type of fabric, like a "space blanket", which reflects heat back to your body. It is sandwiched between nylon on the outside and soft polyester on the inside. It functions well when wet, and is easy to clean.

The final type of undergarment is made of Thinsulate®, which is usually coated with nylon on the outside, and soft cotton or polyester on the inside. It is a very good insulator, even when wet. It is relatively thin, breathable, and very comfortable. It is also fair-

Fig. 3.13 –*Dry gloves are bulky, but very warm, see diver on right; (photo D. Bockus)*

ly expensive. Thinsulate ®must be laundered carefully, according to the manufacturers instructions.

Some divers wear a thin wet suit under the dry suit, and report that it keeps them sufficiently warm.

Weight and Buoyancy Systems

Dry suits require a considerable amount of weight to be worn to achieve neutral buoyancy. However, there is a common misconception that diving dry means adding tremendous amounts of weight to the belt. Depending upon the diver's physical characteristics, the type of dry suit, the type of cylinder used, and the type and thickness of undergarments, many divers only add a small amount of weight to achieve neutral buoyancy.

The proper way to use a dry suit is with the minimal amount of air inside the suit necessary to avoid a squeeze. Divers that put excessive amounts of air in the dry suit require more weight than would otherwise be needed. This can lead to buoyancy problems during the dive.

Fig. 3.14 *—Thick 3-fingered mitts with a long gauntlet*

Fig. 3.15 –
*Long underwear
are often worn
underneath the
dive wear for
extra warmth*

Standard weight belts, with lead weights of various sizes, will work with a dry suit. Depending upon the dry suit and undergarments, these type of weights may dig into the dry suit and the diver's hips and create discomfort. Soft weight belts which are filled with lead shot mold to the diver's body, and are more comfortable. They are also easier on the dry suit material.

To achieve proper buoyancy and trim characteristics, many divers redistribute some of their weight onto different parts of the body. One way to accomplish this is by the use of ankle weights. These one to two pound lead shot soft weights clip to each ankle, and help to keep the feet from rising higher than the divers head.

Another method of moving the weight around is by use of a weight and trim system. This weight belt incorporates shoulder straps which transfer the weight onto the divers shoulders, which helps to relieve lower back strain. The harness allows adjustment of the weights forwards, backwards, up, and down to keep the center of gravity below the center of buoyancy. Weights can be dropped or removed by using two quick release mechanisms.

The other part of any weight system is the buoyancy compensator. A buoyancy compensator should always be used with a dry suit to facilitate surface swimming if in open water, and to be used in case the dry suit cannot hold air, the inflator valve malfunctions, or the dry suit totally floods with water. Many dry suit divers prefer a back-type B.C., as it does not cover-up or interfere with the dry suit valves. Special care should be exercised when using a power inflator in freezing water. Only short bursts should be used to avoid freeze-up and free flow.

Fig. 3.16 –
Thinsulate® *undergarments work well even if wet*

Care and Maintenance

Proper care and maintenance of your dry suit will prolong its useful life, and provide many years of warm, comfortable diving. One of the most important steps is to thoroughly rinse the suit and its parts in fresh water after diving. If possible, have your buddy rinse you down with a garden hose while you are still in the suit. This keeps water from getting inside.

Use caution when removing a dry suit in freezing weather, as the zipper can become stiff and brittle. Open the zipper carefully and entirely. To remove a latex neck seal, reach through the top of the seal with both hands and spread the neck seal open. Lift the seal up and over the head. Be careful not to let fingernails dig into the seal. For a neoprene neck seal, first unroll the seal, then use the same method. To remove wrist seals, you can pull your hand out by turning the sleeve inside out, or you or your buddy can spread the seal open while you pull your hand through.

After you have removed the dry suit, close the zipper, and hold the wrist seals together with the neck seal, in a position above the rest of the suit. This way water will not get inside the suit while

Fig. 3.17 –*Soft weight belt*

Fig. 3.18 –*Ankle weights are useful to keep the legs from floating up above the head*

rinsing. Rinse the valves and zipper thoroughly. Blow the valves dry with compressed air after rinsing. If your suit got wet inside during the dive, it should be rinsed as well.

Latex seals should be washed occasionally with a dilute solution of soapy water to remove body oils. It is best to hang the suit upside down in a shady area to dry, with the zipper open. Never hang your suit in the sun to dry, as this can damage the material. If the inside of the suit is wet, turn it inside out all the way to the boots and allow the inside to dry. Feel down into the boots to make sure it is dry.

When the suit is dry, the latex seals should be talcum-powdered to keep them from sticking.

The zipper is an important and expensive part of a dry suit. It requires proper care and maintenance to perform properly and last many years. Lubricating with wax has already been discussed. Anytime the zipper teeth become dirty, they should be cleaned with a toothbrush and soapy water before the zipper is opened or closed. Use care when closing the zipper, as undergarments that may get caught in the zipper can cause damage to the teeth. If zipper teeth become out of alignment or broken, they should be

Fig. 3.19 –*Proper trim is important for buoyancy control in a dry suit*

checked by a dealer prior to use. Check with the manufacturer for storage suggestions. Generally, the suit should be stored with the zipper open.

Dry suits should be clean and dry before storage. The zipper should be open to avoid excessive compression on the sealing surfaces. Some manufacturers supply a protective cap to place over the inflator valve, to keep the stem from puncturing the suit. Most suits should be rolled up and placed in a bag for storage. These are usually supplied by the manufacturer of the dry suit.

Service and Repairs

Eventually your suit will require service and repairs. The dry suit valves should be inspected and serviced according to manufacturers instructions, which are usually every year. The valves should only be disassembled and repaired by factory trained technicians.

Simple repairs such as small punctures can often be performed by the user. Most manufacturers supply repair kits which contain glues and materials to match the type of dry suit that needs repair.

Replacement of seals can be more difficult, and is best left to a qualified technician. Manufacturers can perform leak tests to determine the source of water leaks in the dry suit.

To locate puncture holes yourself, you can close off the seals with bottles or cans and rubber bands, close the zipper, and fully inflate the suit. Larger holes or split seams can often be identified by listening carefully for escaping air. You can also brush on a dilute solution of soapy water and look for bubbles to form. Another method is to hold sections of the dry suit up to a bright light and look for holes. Mark punctures with a crayon or grease pencil.

Minor field patches can be applied on the inside of nylon fabric materials. Vulcanized rubber suits can often be permanently patched in as little as 10 minutes.

Fig. 3.20 –
DUI Weight/trim
system and har-
ness combination

Cylinders and Valve Configurations

Ice diving requires a sufficient supply of air to complete the intended dive, plus a reserve amount of air for potential emergencies. An 80 to 100 cubic foot cylinder should be considered the minimum volume for the primary cylinder. It should be equipped with a "Y" or "H" valve configuration, to allow for mounting two independent regulators on a single cylinder.

Modular valve systems can be expanded to change configurations as the diver requires. A basic K valve can be adapted to convert to an H valve, allowing for the attachment of primary and backup regulators. Either regulator can be independently isolated if there is a malfunction. Double cylinder configurations can also be incorporated with these valve systems.

A secondary scuba cylinder, or pony bottle, which is a small, approximately 15 cubic foot cylinder, can be used with its own separate regulator in place of the valve configuration described above.

O-rings can become brittle in freezing conditions. They should be cleaned and lubricated often, and inspected for cracks.

Fig. 3.21 –*Some buoyancy compensators have integral D-rings that are strong enough to be used for tethering*

Fig. 3.22 –
The buoyancy compensator should not block access to the dry suit valves

Regulators

Double hose regulators were utilized in many of the early ice dives, but are generally not used today. They work well in freezing water, but are not manufactured any longer, and parts are difficult to find for the older models. Many modern single hose scuba regulators will not function well in cold or freezing water. Both the first and second stages can freeze. First stage freezing can occur due to the expansion that takes place when air leaves the cylinder. This lowers the temperature of the air and hence the first stage body, and can cause any water inside the first stage regulator to freeze. This can hamper the movement of the spring operated first stage valve. Some regulators have environmental kits which fill the space surrounding the first stage spring with an anti-freeze glycol or silicone solution. A diaphragm or rubber cap contains the anti-freeze while still allowing the ambient pressure to be transferred to the first stage mechanism.

Fig. 3.23 –
*Care should be
taken when
removing a
dry suit in
cold weather*

The second stage regulator can also freeze-up in very cold temperatures. Any moisture in the second stage, including the moisture in exhaled air, can freeze, and the ice can jam the lever controlling the valve.

The Sherwood Maximus regulator has been shown to function extremely well in the sub-zero water temperatures in Antarctica. This is due to the design of the first stage, which has an overpressure bleed valve that keeps the freezing water from contacting the spring inside the regulator body. This regulator also has gold plated fins in the second stage which capture the heat of the diver's exhaled air and conduct it to the second stage mechanism, which prevents it from freezing.

To avoid regulator malfunctions, regulators must be cared for properly before, during, and after diving. Regulators should be kept dry and warm before the dive. Care should be taken to avoid breathing on the regulator before submersion, except to briefly ensure it is functioning. The diver can inhale on the regulator, and exhale after removing the regulator from the mouth. This will keep the moisture in the exhaled breath from freezing up in the second stage in very cold weather.

During a dive, if the primary regulator freezes up and free flows, the diver should switch to the back-up regulator, and turn off the valve to the primary regulator to stop the free flow. A regulator should never be used to fill a lift bag, as the rapid movement of air will usually cause a free flow problem to develop.

After diving, care should be taken when rinsing a regulator, especially if it is to be used again soon. Any fresh water remaining in the first or second stage can freeze up when exposed to cold ambient temperatures.

Fig. 3.24 – *The valves and zipper must be rinsed thoroughly*

Tips on Keeping Water Out of Regulators

Always open the cylinder valve briefly before mounting the regulator, to blow out any moisture from the orifice.

When purging the regulator for removal, hold the second stage lower than the first stage so that water cannot drip back to the first stage after the pressure has dropped.

Remove the regulator carefully, so as not to allow ice or water to fall onto the filter of the regulator.

Dry the dust cap thoroughly before attaching it to the regulator.

The dust cap must fit snugly before rinsing the regulator.

Do not depress the purge button while rinsing.

Shake excess water from the second stage before hanging the regulator to dry.

Dive Knife, Mask, and Fins

A knife is mandatory equipment for each diver, as the potential for entanglement during ice diving is always present. Many divers prefer to carry a small, sharp knife to use to cut fishing line or other lines that they might become entangled in. The knife should be located in an area not subjected to suit squeeze as this will cause straps to loosen and the knife sheath to move around. Many divers place the knife on the buoyancy compensator or the regulator console.

The type of dive mask used is not critical. It is best to avoid spitting into the mask for defogging, as this can freeze onto the inside of the face plate in cold weather. Commercial defogging agents work well for ice diving. Straps also can become brittle in cold weather, and spares should be available at the dive site.

The foot pockets of the fins needs to be sufficiently large to accommodate the attached boots on most dry suits.

Fig. 3.25 –*The zipper must be lubricated occasionally with wax*

Fig. 3.26 –*Minor suit repairs can be done by the user*

Instruments, Gauges, and Computers

Some electronic instruments will not function well in sub-freezing temperatures. Liquid crystal displays may be slow to display due to the cold ambient temperature. Plastics can become very brittle and can shatter under freezing conditions, so care should be taken to avoid rough treatment of instruments housed in plastic.

Batteries in dive computers and other instruments will also run low sooner in cold temperatures. Spare batteries should be carried for models that allow user replacement.

Dive Lights

If the conditions are very dark under the ice, divers should use a minimum of two lights per diver. Small mini-lights are good for a back-up in case of primary light failure. A powerful primary underwater light will brighten the way and make an ice dive more enjoyable. There are a number of different types of lights and batteries available which suit different purposes.

A back-up light should be compact and lightweight. Several flashlight-size models are available which weigh less than one

Fig. 3.27 *–a "Y" valve allows the attachment of two independent regulators to one cylinder*

pound. They will not have the intensity or beam angle of a larger light, but their advantage is in their compact size. A primary dive light is somewhat larger than a back-up light. It will have greater power and a larger beam angle than smaller compact lights. They are also heavier and require more batteries. A typical hand-held dive light weighs about five pounds on land.

A stretchable or adjustable lanyard should be attached to your dive light to prevent loss. The stretchable or adjustable feature is important so your hand can pull free in case the light becomes caught. Some lights float and others sink. The ideal light for ice diving would be slightly positively buoyant, and float with the beam pointing down. This would make it easier to recover if lost.

Chemical light sticks, or a small single-battery marker light, can be attached to your gauge console or cylinder valve to make it easy for you and your buddy to keep track of one another. They can also be used as a backup for signaling in case the primary light fails. The chemical light tube contains two separate chemicals. When the tube is bent, thin glass inside breaks and allows the chemicals to mix, which produces a glow that can last several hours. They are available in a variety of sizes and colors, which can be useful for identifying different groups of divers, or dive leaders.

Surface Supplied Diving

Surface supplied diving, with a hose delivering air and hard wire communications to the diver, is generally considered to be beyond the capabilities of normal recreational diving. However, it does have particular advantages when used for under ice diving, such as the primary and backup air supplies are controlled by the topside tender, and the presence of voice communications generally improve the safety of the dive.

As an intermediary between traditional scuba diving and the more commercial-oriented surface supplied diving, some dive teams are using tethered scuba diving. This is essentially a line-tended scuba diving mode utilizing full face masks with communications and redundant scuba. This type of diving deviates from the traditional buddy diving concept of recreational diving and uses only one diver in the water at a time, and should only be attempted by those with proper training and equipment, such as rescue or scientific divers. Full face masks can also be used with traditional scuba, and have the advantage of providing diver to diver and diver to surface communications, as well as providing more thermal protection to the diver's face.

Fig. 3.28 –*Two independent regulators mounted on a cylinder*

Fig. 3.29 –*Diver using a double hose regulator*

Safety Harness and Lines

An adjustable chest harness made of nylon webbing is used to attach a safety line to the diver. It is worn over the exposure suit and under the scuba unit. The safety line is connected to the harness with a locking caribiner.

A safety line is required equipment for all under-ice diving. It is used for line pull communications signals with the surface tender, for relocating the entry/exit hole in low visibility conditions, and for safety in situations if a current occurs during a dive.

The safety line should be constructed of strong synthetic material such as polypropylene or nylon, and should be approximately 1/4 inch (7 mm) in diameter. Another commonly used line is 3/8 inch (10-11 mm) non-floating polypropylene line. Kernmantle rope is constructed of a high strength inner core surrounded by an abrasion resistant outer sheath. The heavier the line, the more drag and difficulty the diver will have in manipulating and giving and receiving signals when it is extended. Thin lines tend to tangle more easily. Brightly colored line is available and easy to see underwater.

Fig. 3.30 –*Poseidon environmental cap on first stage regulator (top right) and ice formation on first stage regulator (left) (photo by Terry Rioux)*

Some ropes have better abrasion resistance, which will increase the useable life of the line. Some lines are coated to prevent water absorption, which keeps the lines lighter in weight. Ropes are also prone to deterioration by ultraviolet sunlight and certain chemicals (see Table 3.1).

The safety line should be no longer than 150 feet (45 m), and marked off in increments of 25 feet (8 m). The marks can be made with tape and permanent markers, or with cable ties. The line should be stored in a rope bag or 5 gallon plastic bucket to keep it dry and free from entanglement. Ideally, the line should be stored long-term in a clean, dry, dark area. Lines should be inspected periodically for signs of wear, which are characterized by fading, brittleness, crumbling fibers, abrasion, or cuts.

On the diver's end of the safety line, a loop is tied using a figure eight knot. This loop is secured to the diver's safety harness using a locking caribiner. The other end of the safety line is secured at the surface to an ice screw or other stationary object that will not be moved, and that cannot wear or sever the line.

Table 3.1. **Line materials, strength, and resistance to chemicals and U/V sunlight.**

Type of Line	Strength	Resistance to Oils/ Greases	Resistance to U/V Sunlight
Nylon	Strongest most resilient	Very good to good	Good
Polyester	Strong Resilient	Very good to good	Good to excellent
Polyolefins (polypropylene)	Strong Moderate resilience	Very good	Fair. UV Inhibitors can be added
Polyethylene	Lowest of all synthetics	Good to very good	Fair. UV stabilizers can be added
Manila	Low strength /weight ratio	Poor	Fair

The standby diver will use a floating type of line, which is usually made of polypropylene. It should be of a bright color different than the diver's lines, and be at least 50% longer than the diver's lines.

Care should be taken to avoid allowing line to become frozen by leaving it lying on the ice. This can weaken the line. It is also important to avoid stepping on the lines. It should be played in and out of the storage container (i.e. stacked or flaked) as the diver ascends and descends.

Thermal Protection for Surface Personnel

Ice diving operations entail many hours of labor on the surface, ranging from hard work shoveling, digging, and sawing, to stationary standing while tending a diver underwater. The weather conditions can range from relatively mild to very cold with wind or snow. For these reasons, surface personnel should be equipped with warm waterproof clothing. By layering clothing, one can adapt to the range of conditions and level of activity. There are many excellent synthetic fabrics such as polypropylene and Capilene® and others that can be worn next to the skin to wick moisture away from the body. Another layer of wool or sweaters, or synthetic insulating materials such as Thinsulate®, Qualofil®, or pile can be worn next, followed by waterproof yet breathable outerwear shell pants and jacket made of Gore-Tex®, Thintech®, or Ultrex®. Down is very warm, yet loses its insulative value when wet, which is likely when working around water and ice.

A good pair of waterproof boots with liners are essential for working on the ice. Waterproof overboots or gaiters can also be

Fig. 3.31 –*The back-up regulator must be readily accessible in the chest area of the diver*

Fig. 3.32 –
*Special care
should be given
to electronic
instruments
used in cold
water*

used to keep the boots dry. Crampons can be attached to the boots to facilitate walking on slippery ice.

A couple pairs of gloves or mittens with wool or synthetic liners are a must. The gloves will get wet when handling lines and dive equipment, and an extra pair kept warm in an inside pocket are essential. Remember also that tenders will be touching alot of metal parts, which conduct heat away from the hands and can be dangerous if handled with bare hands. A great deal of heat can be lost through the head, and a balaclava, or hat made of synthetic material or wool should be worn. Sunglasses should be worn if the tenders will spend long periods in bright conditions on the snow and ice.

Fig. 3.33 –*A dive light is extremely useful under the ice (photo J. Brooks)*

Emergency Equipment

Depending upon the location and circumstances of the dive, you will have to decide upon the type of emergency equipment to have on site, and what you will rely on rescue personnel to provide. Some type of communications equipment must be on site or nearby. These include a telephone or mobile radio. It is wise to have oxygen and personnel trained in its use at the dive site. Precious minutes can be lost waiting for rescue personnel to arrive. A standard first aid kit and extra blankets or a sleeping bag are also a necessity.

Additional Equipment

In addition to all of the equipment discussed above, additional equipment may be required. Surface personnel should consider wearing a personal flotation device (PFD) in case of accidental immersion in the water. Dive lights and photographic equipment require fresh batteries or recharge, and should be kept warm during diving preparations. Batteries will lose their power much more rapidly at lower temperatures.

Some mountaineering equipment may be required, depending upon the dive site. An ice ax or pick is handy for evaluating ice conditions and for use when walking or hiking on ice, especially if there are any slopes to be negotiated. Ice screws are useful for securing safety lines to the ice if no other strong, immovable object is located nearby. Hollow, tubular ice screws or snargs are desirable as they can be placed into the ice with a minimum of ice displacement or shattering. Ice is displaced into the center of the screw as it is placed. Ice pitons can be driven into the ice and used as well. Locking caribiners are useful for securing lines to the diver. Shovels, tarps, and pallets are also useful. All of this equipment can be transported to the dive site on a sled or toboggan, which can be pulled behind people, or towed behind a snowmobile.

Fig. 3.34 –
Surface supplied diving (photo D. Andersen)

Fig. 3.35 –
AGA full-face masks can be used for ice diving, with the proper training

Fig. 3.36 –
The harness is worn over the suit and under the cylinder and buoyancy compensator

Fig. 3.37 –*Tethers are available in a variety of colors, materials, and thicknesses*

Fig. 3.38 –
Tender paying out the tether line

Fig. 3.39 – *Tenders must wear proper clothing to stay warm during diving operations (photo D. Bockus)*

Fig. 3.40 – *Waterproof boots and gloves are most important*

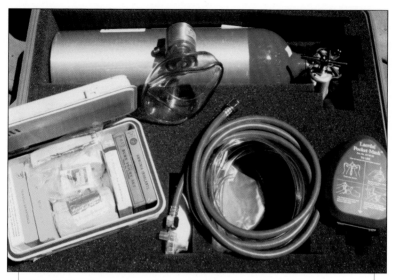

Fig. 3.41 – *An oxygen and first aid kit are desirable equipment to have on-site*

Fig. 3.42 –
A radio or cellular telephone can be used for emergency communications

Chapter 4

Ice Diving
Operations

Ice diving is an incredibly time and labor intensive activity. It takes a relatively large group of people and a considerable amount of time, to find a suitable diving location, evaluate the ice conditions, prepare the site, review the dive plan, conduct the dive, and pack up to leave the site.

Evaluating Ice Conditions

For ice diving operations, the ice must be of sufficient thickness and strength to support the entire dive team, and possibly vehicles or snowmobiles as well. A minimum thickness of 6 inches (15 cm) is required for small groups. Vehicles should only be driven onto ice of at least 12 inches (30 cm) thickness. New, early winter ice, or older spring melt ice may be particularly weak. Caution should be used when venturing out onto this type of ice.

To evaluate the ice conditions, two people are required. One should be dressed in a dry suit and equipped with a harness and safety line, and have an ice pick or ice ax. This person will advance slowly out onto the ice, followed by the safety person who is well behind. Ice thickness can be measured using an auger (drill) or ice pick. Some groups use gasoline powered post hole digging augers (4 inch or 10 cm diameter). A graduated, marked measuring staff with a bent tip can be inserted through the hole and hooked under the ice, so that an accurate measurement of ice thickness can be made. The ice thickness should initially be measured close to shore, as ice is often thickest near shore. If it is of sufficient thickness, then the team can carefully venture out to the anticipated dive location.

In marine situations, the fast-ice cover creates a wave-free and surge-free location for diving. However, there are often cracks and pressure ridges in the ice due to tidal action and currents.

Fig. 4.1 —*Ice diving requires considerable preparation before the dive (photo J. Nickel)*

These cracks can be used with caution to gain access to the water. In pack-ice, the broken ice cover eliminates the need to open an access hole. However, this type of ice is unstable and can move quickly with changing surface conditions. The surface tenders and divers must constantly monitor conditions for safety.

Preparing The Site

Once the ice thickness has been measured, it is a good idea to measure the bottom depth. This can be done by lowering a measured shot line with a light lead weight to the bottom.

Some type of surface shelter is also desirable, to provide heating and shelter from the wind and elements. This can be in the form of a van, trailer, cabin, or tents. To minimize the chance of slipping on the ice, you can sprinkle sand or gravel around the dive hole area. Surface personnel and divers will stay warmer if their boots are not in contact with the ice. Sheets of plywood or insulating pads can be used for this purpose.

Fig. 4.2 –
*A test hole must
be drilled
through the ice*

There are a number of different ways to gain access to the water through the ice. If the ice is relatively thin (up to about 3 feet, or 1m), the ice can be cut by hand using a handsaw, pick, or chainsaw. It is helpful to move the hole cutting equipment out to the dive site in a toboggan or on a sled, rather than carrying it.

There are several options regarding the shape of the dive hole. Most divers use a triangular "hole", as this requires one less cut than a square or rectangular hole. The corner angles also make it comfortable for entries and exits. The size of the hole should be large enough to accommodate two divers and a safety diver at the same time. This requires a hole of about five to six feet on a side.

The actual cutting of the ice requires the use of hand saws, breaker bars/chippers, and/or chain saws. Surface personnel should wear waterproof clothing to minimize getting wet and cold. It is easiest to drill the corners of the hole with an auger, and then cut from corner to corner through about 90% of the ice with a chain saw, in order to minimize splashing water onto the operator of the chain saw. The actual cut into the corner holes and through the remaining ice is done last by hand with the ice saw, or with the chain saw.

Ice is extremely heavy, and removal from the hole can be difficult. Some dive teams place an ice screw in the center of the ice block, to which a line is attached. The ice block can then be pushed under the surrounding ice to keep it safely away from the hole during the diving operations. The line allows for replacement of the block after the diving is completed. Another method is to drill a hole through the ice about eight feet from one side of the triangle, and to drill another through the center of the ice block, and one more on the edge. The block can be pushed under the ice, lining up the holes, and a rod with a line attached can be pushed through both holes in the ice, securing the block to the frozen ice surface. A line can be passed through the extra hole on the edge of the block in order to pull it back into the hole at the end of the diving day.

Fig. 4.3 –*Cracks in sea ice are common and must be carefully evaluated (photo D. Bockus)*

Fig. 4.4 –*A heated shelter, like this trailer, is essential for safety (photo J. McClintock)*

Some divers prefer to open one or more additional safety holes that can be used by divers in an emergency. All holes in the ice should be clearly marked so that surface personnel and others will not fall into them. Bamboo poles with bright colored flags work well for this purpose. Floating anchor ice and platelet ice dislodged by divers can fill up a dive hole. It must be cleared by tenders using a dip net.

Underwater visibility can often be improved by removing snow cover from the surface of the ice. One method of aiding divers underwater in locating the dive hole is to shovel radiating lines from the hole much like spokes of a wheel. "V" 's can be shoveled along each line pointing to the direction of the hole.

Chemical lights, or small flashing strobe lights can be hung on a line underwater to help divers in locating the hole while underwater. An effective method of diver recall is to place a piece of metal such as a shovel or iron bar in the water, and strike it with a hammer.

Fig. 4.5 –*A tent can be erected as a shelter. Here hot air is blown into the tent by a large heater (photo J. McClintock)*

Dive Planning and Personnel

Ice diving requires extensive planning and a number of personnel to be done correctly. Before preparations for the dive begin, the weather conditions must be evaluated. A weather forecast will help to determine if conditions are expected to deteriorate or improve. If the forecast or current conditions indicate bad weather such as heavy winds, an approaching storm, or extreme cold, the dive should be postponed or canceled.

Each diver should have a separate tether line and tender, but the divers must use care not to tangle the lines during the dive. As an alternative, both divers can be controlled by one tender using a "Y" line. This type of tether branches into a "Y" at the divers end, with each diver having about a 6 foot length of line off the main tether.

The dive tender is one of the most important members of the diving operation. This person should preferably be a trained ice diver, and helps to assemble equipment, and essentially dresses the diver into his equipment on the surface. While the divers are

Fig. 4.6 –*A snowmobile or sled can be used to transport equipment to the dive site*

Fig. 4.7 –*Snow must be shoveled from the ice before cutting (photo J. Nickel)*

Fig. 4.8 –*A qualified person cuts the ice with a chain saw*

Fig. 4.9 –*A triangular cut block of ice is ready to be moved (photo J. Nickel)*

Fig. 4.10 –
*Extra safety holes
can be opened for
emergency use
(photo D. Bockus)*

underwater, the tender pays out the safety line, and keeps in contact with the diver(s) by use of line pull signals. The tender must keep in constant contact with the safety line while the divers are underwater. Tenders must be warm in order to function well during the dive. Waterproof gloves, boots, and warm insulated clothing and headgear are essential for tenders. Some tenders use cramp-on spikes on their boots for more solid footing around the dive hole.

A safety diver must be suited up and ready to enter the water with little notice while divers are in the water. The safety diver usually has all equipment on and in place, except for cylinder/buoyancy compensator, and mask and fins. The safety diver must be kept warm, and all equipment must be functional and ready to go if called for. An additional person is desirable to help with surface equipment, and is especially helpful in an emergency to call for help, assist the safety diver, and assist divers in exiting the water.

Fig. 4.11 –*The dive hole can be cleaned with a shovel,*

Fig. 4.12 –*or a dip net and ice tongs, if significant chunks of ice are present*

The dive plan should be discussed before the divers suit up. Line signals should be reviewed with the tenders. Signals should be simple and well understood by all participants. The tender should keep the line taught, without hindering the diver's movements. A common rule is for the tender to give one pull every five minutes to check if everything is OK. A briefing on the objective of the dive, maximum depth and underwater time, tasks and responsibilities, distance to be traveled from the dive hole, any physical or biological hazards, and emergency procedures must be reviewed by all personnel on site.

Table 4.1. Line pull signals.

Line Pull Signal	Tender to Diver	Diver to Tender
1 Pull	Are you OK?	I am OK
2 Pulls	Do you need more line?	I need more line
3 Pulls	No line remaining	Take in slack
4 Pulls	Come up now!	Emergency! Pull me Back!
Many repeated pulls		Help! Send safety diver!

Diving at Altitude

Ice diving might be conducted at altitude, which may require additional planning due to the remoteness of the site, the terrain, and decompression and instrument calibration considerations. Sea level decompression tables are generally only useable up to an altitude of 1000 feet (330 m). Training in altitude diving should be completed in open water before altitude ice diving is considered.

Suiting Up

The divers should suit up in a place that is protected from the outside weather. Places such as inside a heated tent, a motorhome or trailer, or a cabin are all acceptable. This may be some distance from the actual dive site. Divers can be transported to the dive site by snowmobile or vehicle if necessary.

All equipment should be kept warm before the dive. This is especially true for regulators which can freeze-up, especially in cold air conditions. They should be kept dry, as any water in the regulator can freeze in the cold air, causing a free flow situation. If a regulator will be used on more than one dive during a day, they can be kept in warm water in an ice chest between dives.

The tenders duties before the dive are to assist the divers in donning their equipment. One reason for this is to allow the divers to wear their land gloves so that their hands will stay warm. When the divers have their dry suits on and are ready for diving, the tenders help them into their harnesses and weight belts. The divers then sit at the edge of the ice hole, where the tenders assist them in donning their buoyancy compensators, cylinders, gloves, fins and

Fig. 4.13 –*Spokes can be shoveled in the snow, (photo N. Langerman)*

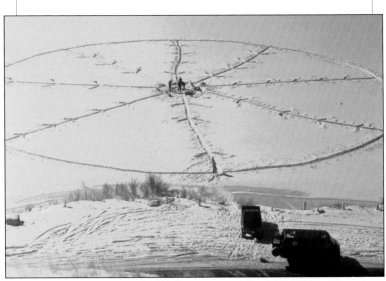

Fig. 4.14 –
to provide direction toward the hole to the divers below (photo N. Langerman)

mask. The tether line is attached to the diver's harness. The regulators are properly routed and secured, including the redundant regulator, and all power inflators are connected. Both cylinder valves (primary and redundant) are opened.

The diver's gloves are extremely important, as the hands tend to become cold first during a dive. If dry gloves are used, care should be taken to assure a correct seal on the cuff rings. Divers using wet gloves often have the tenders pour warm water from a thermos into the gloves prior to donning them.

As part of the final buddy check, the divers and tenders check that all of the equipment is properly placed and functional. One exception to this is the scuba regulator. It is important to not breathe from the regulator in the air before the dive, as this can cause a freeze-up and free flow situation. The divers should place the regulator in the mouth loosely just prior to entering the water, and breathe around the mouthpiece until in the water. Once the regulator is immersed in the water, normal breathing through the regulator can be done.

The Dive

The best entry to use is a seated entry at a corner of the hole, where the diver places both hands on one side and rotates around on the hands to slip into the water feet first. Both divers should descend slightly and test their regulators and lights, then descend together and maintain visual contact with each other. Air should only be added to the dry suit in short bursts of no more than one second to avoid a valve freeze-up.

Care should be taken to avoid contact with the bottom, especially if it is silty, so that the sediment is not kicked up, thereby

Fig. 4.15–
*Tethered diver
prepares to enter
the water*

reducing the water visibility. The divers should also avoid cross-
ing over each other's tether lines to avoid entanglement.

The tender and diver will communicate frequently using the
line pull signals shown in Table 4.1. The tender must always have
control of the tether line during the dive. The diver should hold
the line in one hand in order to feel the line pull signals.

The divers should descend to the predetermined maximum
depth early in the dive, and proceed to work their way shallower
during the dive. The tenders will feed rope out of the rope bag as
needed by the divers. A maximum distance of about 100 feet from
the dive hole is normally allowed. The divers should monitor
depth, underwater time, and air pressure frequently during the
dive. The tenders will monitor surface weather conditions during
the dive.

Air management is critical in this overhead environment type
of diving. The prudent diver will use the rule of thirds, where one-

Fig. 4.16 –
*Safety diver is
suited up and
ready if needed*

Fig. 4.17 –*Ice diving is often conducted in mountain lakes at altitude (photo by John Nickel)*

third of the air supply is used for descent and excursion to the maximum distance from the hole, the next third is used to return to the dive hole, and the remaining third is saved for emergencies. It is important to carry enough gas to breathe if the dive hole is lost and a safety diver must commence a search. Divers must also have a reserve supply of gas sufficient enough for the safety decompression stop.

Divers can become very cold while ice diving. With proper insulation under the dry suit, the body will stay quite warm. However, the hands and lips are usually the first areas to get cold. If the lips become so cold that the diver cannot hold the regulator in his mouth, then he should hold the regulator in place manually and end the dive. The hands are also very susceptible to cold. If they become cold or numb, to the point that dexterity is compromised, the dive must be concluded immediately.

Divers may become disconcerted if the visibility is less than the distance from them to the entry/exit hole. If there is any anxiety, then the divers should return to within sight of the hole. At the end of the dive, divers can ascend either diagonally by following the line back to the hole, or horizontally along the bottom until

Fig. 4.18 –*Tenders help divers don all equipment (photo J. Nickel)*

underneath the hole, and then making a vertical ascent. A safety stop of 3 to 5 minutes at a depth of about 15 feet is recommended.

When the divers surface, they will often be cold, especially the hands, and may be unable to manipulate their equipment efficiently. The tender should always assist the diver out of the water. Equipment such as weight belts or the B.C. and cylinder can be removed while the diver is in the water, if necessary. The low pressure inflator hose may have to be removed from the dry suit by the tender. While one diver is removing their equipment and exiting the hole, the other diver should stay clear of the hole in case equipment is dropped. The divers should proceed to the warm shelter for rewarming and removal of the rest of the equipment, while the tenders secure the equipment and the area around the dive hole.

Surface personnel can switch places with the divers after everyone has had a chance to rest, warm up, and review the dive.

Fig. 4.19 –
*Tender pours
hot water into
diver's gloves*

Fig. 4.20 –
*Entry can be
made from a
seated position
on the ice (photo
J. Nickel)*

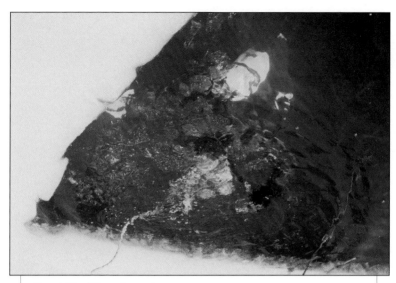

Fig. 4.21 –*Diver descends*

Fig. 4.22 –*Care should be taken to avoid tangling tether lines (photo J. Nickel)*

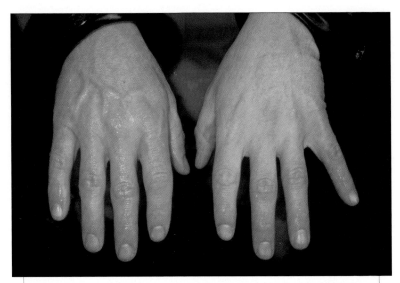

Fig. 4.23 – *Diver's hands can become cold very quickly and should be monitored by the diver*

Fig. 4.24 –
A safety stop should be made at the end of every dive

Fig. 4.25 –*The diver may have to be helped onto the ice by the tender after the dive (photo J. Nickel)*

Fig. 4.26 –*Tenders help remove diver's gear*

Fig. 4.27 –*The site must be well-marked before leaving it*

Fig. 4.28 –*Tenders hauling gear back to shore (photo J. McClintock)*

Chapter 5

Safety and Emergency Procedures

Safety is of paramount importance in all ice diving operations. As in all types of diving, the prevention of problems is obviously preferable to having to solve them under adverse conditions. Emergency procedures should be practiced and be well understood by all participants in ice diving.

Environmental Hazards

There are certain environmental hazards that should be evaluated and considered by cold water and ice divers. Currents can be especially dangerous when diving in or under an ice cover. The existence of a current can be established by lowering a weighted line (about 2-3 lbs.; 1-2 kg.) into the water and checking for deflection in the current. Small streamers or flags can also be tied to the line to check for currents at various depths, if the water visibility permits. Diving in currents greater than 0.5 knot (approx. 25 cm/sec) is not recommended.

Another potential danger of currents and wind in ocean ice diving situations is moving ice. Small pieces of ice to large icebergs can pin divers to the bottom, or block an exit point. Surface personnel must be attentive to moving ice, and be prepared to recall the divers to the surface if necessary.

Blowing wind and moving ice are also extremely important when diving from a boat. Divers and boat drivers can become chilled easily when winds blow across ice and water. Some type of insulation from the wind should be utilized, ranging from a windproof overcoat to a sheltered cabin. Care must be taken to assure that a safe passage back to shore is not blocked by moving ice.

Underwater visibility can be very good in some ice diving conditions. It can range from spectacular 600 foot (180 m) visibility in the Antarctic, to 60 foot (18 m) visibility in some lakes, to zero visi-

Fig. 5.1 – *An extensive amount of safety equipment may be required when diving in remote areas*

bility in plankton blooms, silty conditions, or where the ice is very thick and has a considerable cover of snow.

Diving within visual sight of the dive hole is comforting for most people. However, with a secure tether and communication with a buddy and surface tender, diving can continue beyond visual distance of the dive hole as long as other safety procedures are adhered to.

It is important for divers to avoid stirring up a silty bottom, which can reduce the visibility to zero. Proper buoyancy control, and the use of a cave diving type kick, with knees bent and fins up off the bottom, are essential to prevent silt from being re-suspended in the water column.

Aquatic life is not much of a danger in ice diving. In certain marine situations predators such as leopard seals or killer whales may present a problem.

Emergency Procedures

Regulator Freeze-up

Scuba regulators can freeze-up in very cold conditions. To decrease the chance of this happening, regulators should be kept warm and dry before the dive. Very often the air temperature is lower than the water temperature, and breathing on the regulator on the surface should be avoided, as this can easily promote freeze-up and regulator free flow.

A regulator should never be used to fill a lift bag underwater. When large volumes of air are moved through the regulator, freezing and free flow can easily occur. For this reason, many divers attach the low pressure dry suit inflator to the backup regulator, so that excessive demand is not placed on the primary regu-

Fig. 5.2 – *The presence of a current can often be determined by lowering a marked down line (photo by Jim Mastro)*

lator first stage. The inflator can also then be used even if the primary regulator and valve are turned off.

In the case of primary regulator freeze-up or free flow, the diver should switch over to the backup regulator, which should be attached to the buoyancy compensator or safety harness in a readily accessible location. After breathing is established, the cylinder valve supplying the primary regulator should be shut off by the diver or buddy, and the dive must be terminated.

Inflator Valve Malfunction

Inflator valves should be operated in short bursts only, never more than a second or two at a time. Excessive use of the inflator can cause freezing of the mechanism. If the inflator valve becomes stuck open, because of freezing or mechanical failure, air will be added rapidly to the suit. You should immediately disconnect the low pressure inflator hose from the dry suit. Raise your arm to vent air from the suit, manually depressing the valve if necessary. If you are ascending, the volume of air in your dry suit will

Fig. 5.3 – *Moving ice can be a danger to divers (photo Terry Rioux)*

Fig. 5.4 –
*Diving from
small boats in
ice conditions
requires careful
attention to
environmental
conditions
(photo by Terry
Rioux)*

expand rapidly, especially in shallow water. If air is not venting fast enough from the exhaust valve, you can pull open your neck seal, or a wrist seal while holding the arm above your head. This will dump air rapidly, but will also allow some water inside the suit. Of course in a rapid ascent you must exhale nearly continuously to avoid lung overexpansion injuries.

If you cannot put air into the suit using the inflator valve, do not descend any further. You must terminate the dive. If you are neutrally buoyant, begin ascent. You might have to use the B.C. as needed for additional buoyancy.

Dropped or Lost Weight Belt

If you feel your weight belt fall off your body, you should immediately try to grab hold of the belt. Depending upon the

Fig. 5.5 –
*Underwater
visibility can
exceed 500
feet in the
Antarctic*

depth and your buoyancy, you may be able to kick hard towards the bottom to recover the weight belt. As long as you are holding onto the weights, you will not rise rapidly to the surface. Don the weight belt and secure it. If you cannot recover the weight belt, try to grasp anything that you can, such as kelp, a down line, rocks, etc. If you begin rising to the surface in an uncontrolled ascent, vent air out of the suit, and do a horizontal flare to slow the ascent rate. Practice these situations only under the supervision of a qualified instructor.

If you find yourself at the surface under the ice without a weight belt, it will be very difficult for you to maneuver your body. You can signal to the tender with your safety line to haul you in to the hole. You can assist by kicking with your fins and pushing off the ice with your hand. Your buddy should also be aware of your situation and can assist you as needed. As a last resort, the safety diver can be deployed, and can easily follow the trapped diver's safety line to assist the buoyant diver back to the dive hole.

Entanglement

Ice diving typically involves tether lines, down lines, and other items that offer potential for entanglement. If a diver becomes entangled, the first consideration is to not panic. Most entanglements can be easily removed by the diver or the dive buddy. If you feel a line or other entanglement, remain calm, and do not spin around. Feel for the entanglement, and either gently remove it, or signal to your buddy for assistance. It may be necessary to cut free of an entanglement. Before cutting a line, be sure that it is not a tether line or other safety line used in the diving operation.

If a tender finds that a line feels tangled, or gets no response from the diver via line pull signals, then the standby diver must be deployed to investigate the situation. The safety diver can follow the line to the point of entanglement and remedy the problem.

Fig. 5.6 – Green water and limited visibility may be encountered in some frozen lakes (photo by John Nickel)

Flooded Dry Suit

A dry suit can become wet inside through minor leaks in the wrist or neck seals, or through the zipper or other holes in the suit. Minor leaks are annoying but not necessarily hazardous. However, if the dry suit floods completely due to seal failure, zipper failure, or any other reason, the dive must be terminated immediately. Additional buoyancy for ascent may be required through use of the buoyancy compensator. The dry suit should be removed immediately, and the diver rewarmed.

Loss of the Dive Hole

One of the most serious things that can happen during fast ice diving is for the divers to lose the location of the entry/exit hole.

Fig. 5.7 –
*The tether line
is the route back
to the dive hole
in low visibility
conditions
(photo J. Brooks)*

Fig. 5.8 – *In very cold water the first stage regulator can freeze, and if the second stage free flows, it can become packed with ice (photo by Terry Rioux)*

This would only occur if there was a loss of dive tether. If a diver notices that his tether line is lost, his first action should be to locate the line or the dive buddy. If the line is located, communication with the tender should be re-established, the tether reconnected, and the dive terminated. If the line cannot be located, the diver should initiate physical contact with the buddy, and terminate the dive.

If neither the tether nor the buddy can be located, the diver should immediately ascend to under the ice ceiling, and maintain a vertical posture with an arm extended over the head against the ice. This provides the largest possible target for a search procedure. The search procedure requires the safety diver to swim just under the ice in a circular pattern larger than the area the divers were estimated to be from the dive hole. The tether line should catch the lost diver. The lost diver should keep watch below him for the tether line if it passes by below him.

If both divers become disconnected from the surface tethers, they should establish physical contact, ascend slightly, and slowly scan for the tethers in the water column . The divers may be able to retrace their path by following suspended sediments. If this does not produce results, the divers should surface and remain under the ice while the standby diver initiates a search like the one described above. The diver's air supplies will last much longer in shallow water. The surface tender will realize that the line(s) have gone slack, and should immediately lower a brightly colored down line, with strobe flashers if possible, to help the divers locate the access hole.

An alternate method for relocating the dive hole uses technology from cave diving. A lost diver could ascend to under the ice, secure the line from a gap reel to the underside of the ice using a piton or screw, and conduct a circle search for the dive hole in expanding circles. The diver would always be able to return to the starting point, and the simultaneous search by the standby diver could also be accomplished (John Brooks, personal communication).

Fig. 5.9 –
The inflator valve on the dry suit should be depressed in short bursts of only one second duration to avoid freeze-up

Fig. 5.10 – *If the weight belt is dropped or lost, the diver will end up underneath the ice (photo J. Nickel)*

Windchill

Extremes of temperature may be encountered on the surface during diving operations. The tenders must be prepared for cold temperatures, as the effectiveness of the surface personnel may affect the safety of the divers. The wind chill factor can have an effect of much colder air on the skin (see Table 5.1).

People are especially vulnerable to sunburn at higher elevations. In addition, light is reflected from snow and ice, which makes areas such as ears, lips, and eyes particularly vulnerable to sunburn. Sunscreen and lip balm should be worn. Ultraviolet light is present even on cloudy days, and can cause snow blindness. The basic symptoms of snow blindness are extreme pain in the eyes, sore scratchy eyelids, and headache. Treatment is to remove the victim to a dark place. Prevention of this problem is achieved by wearing good quality sunglasses.

Frostbite

Windburn is similar to sunburn, and is caused by cold wind blowing on unprotected skin. It can cause reddening and tender-

Table 5.1. Equivalent Wind Chill Temperature °F (°C)

Wind (mph)	Air Temperatures °F (°C)											
	40(4)	35(2)	30(-1)	25(-4)	20(-7)	15(-9)	10(-12)	5(-15)	0(-17)	-5(-21)	-10(-23)	-15(-26)
5	35(2)	30(-1)	25(-4)	20(-7)	15(-9)	10(-12)	5(-15)	0(-17)	5(-21)	-10(-23)	-15(-26)	-20(-29)
10	30(-1)	20(-7)	15(-9)	10(-12)	5(-15)	0(-17)	-10(-23)	-15(-26)	-20(-29)	-25(-32)	-35(-37)	-40(-40)
15	25(-4)	15(-9)	10(-12)	0(-17)	-5(-21)	-10(-23)	-20(-29)	-25(-32)	-30(-34)	-40(-40)	-45(-43)	-50(-46)
20	20(-7)	10(-12)	5(-15)	0(-17)	-10(-23)	-15(-26)	-25(-32)	-30(-34)	-35(-37)	-45(-43)	-50(-46)	-60(-51)
25	15(-9)	10(-12)	0(-17)	-5(-21)	-15(-26)	-20(-29)	-30(-34)	-35(-37)	-45(-43)	-50(-46)	-60(-51)	-65(-54)
30	10(-12)	5(-15)	0(-17)	-10(-23)	-20(-29)	-25(-32)	-30(-34)	-40(-40)	-50(-46)	-55(-48)	-65(-54)	-70(-60)
35	10(-12)	5(-15)	-5(-21)	-10(-23)	-20(-29)	-30(-34)	-35(-37)	-40(-40)	-50(-46)	-60(-51)	-65(-54)	-75(-60)
40	10(-12)	0(-17)	-5(-21)	-15(-26)	-20(-29)	-30(-34)	-35(-37)	-45(-43)	-55(-48)	-60(-51)	-70(-60)	-75(-60)

Little Danger   Increasing Danger   Great Danger

Fig. 5.11 – *If the diver becomes entangled in the tether line, the buddy must be prepared to assist (photo J. Nickel)*

ness of the skin. Exposed skin should be protected from cold winds.

One result of exposure to cold temperatures is frostbite, which is the freezing of skin or the fluids in the tissues of the skin. The frozen area is usually small, and common areas affected are the nose, cheeks, ears, fingers, and toes. Signs and symptoms of frostbite include white or grayish-yellow skin color, pain sometimes felt, intense cold or numb feeling, and the appearance of blisters. This can progress to more serious symptoms like mental confusion, impairment of judgment, and shock. It is critical to identify the early signs of frostbite and take protective action immediately.

First aid for frostbite includes covering the frozen part, keeping the victim warm, and rewarming the frozen area quickly by immersing it in a warm bath, no warmer than 105 °F. Do not rub the area, as this can cause further damage. Loosely bandage the area with a dry, sterile dressing. Proceed to medical attention as soon as possible.

Hypothermia

The prevention of hypothermia is of foremost concern to everyone involved in ice diving operations. Hypothermia is defined as a lowering of the body core temperature to a stressful level. The central core consists of the brain, spinal cord, chest organs abdomen, and pelvis. The peripheral shell consists of the limbs, muscles, and skin. The core temperature is regulated by the body to remain within narrow limits of the normal body temperature of 98.6 °F (37 °C), while the temperature of the shell can vary considerably. The skin temperature can be considerably lower than normal body temperature, which leads to vasoconstriction, which conserves the core temperature within normal limits.

The transfer of heat occurs between two systems of different temperatures in contact with each other. The larger the gradient, that is the greater the difference in temperature between two

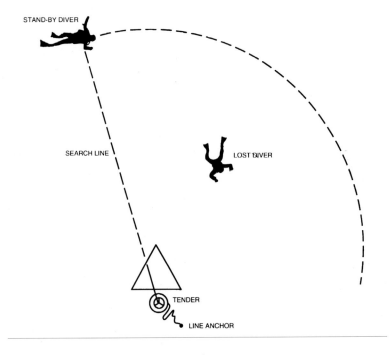

Fig. 5.12 – *Safety diver searching for lost diver*

Fig. 5.13 – *The lost diver should ascend to under the ice, assume a vertical posture, and wait for the safety diver (photo John Nickel)*

items, the higher the rate of heat transfer. One of the Laws of Thermodynamics states that energy (heat) will move from the higher temperature (human body) to the lower temperature water.

Both surface personnel and divers can lose heat through breathing, insufficient thermal insulation, and lack of movement. A loss of as little as 1-2 °F (0.5-1 °C) can result in a loss of mental capacity of 10-20% and as great as a 40% loss of memory. An individual suddenly exposed to very cold water with no thermal protection will often experience immediate disabling effects. As immersion occurs, there is a sudden involuntary inspiration or gasping response which may lead to inhalation of water. This response continues for one to two minutes with an extremely rapid breathing rate which the victim cannot control. As time progresses, there is a decrease in muscle strength, accompanied by pain and mental disorganization, with fear and panic reaction developing.

If the individual has some thermal protection, the immediate effects will not be as severe. Exercise or shivering will increase heat production by increasing the activity of skeletal muscle, but the agitation of water by activity increases heat loss.

Fig. 5.14 – *Wind can drop the ambient temperature considerably*

Exercise increases the heat loss much more at low than high water temperatures and always increases the rate of body heat loss. It is not necessarily futile to try to stay warm with exercise, however. While exercise in the water causes heat loss to the water, contrary to popular belief, you won't always get colder by exercising in the water.

As chilling progresses and the core temperature falls, the individual will show predictable effects which loosely correspond to the core temperature.

Initial symptoms of hypothermia include: sensation of cold, shivering, increased heart rate, urge to urinate, slight incoordination in hand movements. Symptoms will progress to include increasing muscular incoordination, stumbling gait, shivering slows or stops, weakness, apathy, drowsiness, confusion, and slurred speech. In severe hypothermia, where the core temperature is 85-90 °F (29-32 °C), shivering stops, there is inability to walk or follow commands, complaints of loss of vision, and confusion progressing to coma. At a core temperature of 85 °F to 65 °F (29-18 °C) symptoms are muscle rigidity, decreased blood pressure, lowered heart rate and respiration, dilated pupils, and appearance of death.

Fig. 5.15 –
Cold, wet divers can become hypothermic in cold weather conditions

There is some evidence that short-term adaptation can be achieved by individuals in cold climates. A study of divers in the sub-Arctic found improved vasoconstriction, which lead to a reduction in thermal conductance by the tissues, over a period of 45 days.

Management of Heat Loss Victims

Suspecting the existence of hypothermia is the first step in management. Chilling may be mild with little risk to the individual, or severe with a possibility of death. The mildly chilled individual will be awake, complaining of cold, possibly shivering, and able to converse intelligently. The moderately chilled individual will be awake, but may be confused, apathetic or uncooperative, and may have difficulty with speech. If severely chilled or hypothermic, the victim may be unconscious with a slow heart rate and respiration or may even appear dead with no detectable heart beat. The victim who is moderately or severely hypothermic may be made worse or placed in cardiac arrest by careless attempts at re-warming. Hypothermia is an emergency in slow motion and improper handling may actually create a fatal outcome. The cold heart is especially sensitive, and victims alive when found may develop cardiac arrest if handled roughly during the initial evaluation and transportation. The rescuer must transport and re-warm the victim without precipitating cardiac arrest.

Re-warming is of extreme importance, of course, but should not be attempted unless it can be done properly. However, it sometimes becomes necessary to re-warm a chilling victim in an area far from medical care. The first attempts should use passive methods, including protection against further heat loss by removing wet clothing and covering in layers. Do not forget to provide layers between the victim and the ground or deck and to cover the

Fig. 5.16 –
A cold diver can be rewarmed in a variety of ways

head, which is a major source of heat loss. The fully alert and cooperative victim may be given warm liquids to drink; this will deliver negligible amounts of heat, but will help to correct the dehydration. Coffee, tea, caffeine drinks and alcohol should be strictly avoided. Oral fluids may include balanced electrolyte solutions such as Gatorade®, Gastriolyte® or Infalyte®, which are available in powder form. If the victim is awake, s/he should not be exercised because muscular activity will bring cold blood from the periphery to the core. The mildly or moderately chilled victim will soon return to a near normal temperature.

Immersion of the victim in a hot bath was thought to be risky unless limited to the trunk only with the extremities left out. Similarly, body-to-body contact has been limited to bare skin in the trunk area only. Current research indicates that the victim will not have increased cooling of the heart on immersion, limbs and all, in a hot bath.

Fig. 5.17 –
A warm shelter, warm dry clothes, and warm liquids are essential for cold divers

The severely hypothermic victim may be unconscious or appear dead. Look very carefully for signs of life such as breathing, movement or a pulse at the groin or in the neck over the carotid artery. If breathing or movement is present, and the heart is beating, then CPR is not needed. If the breathing rate is six or less per minute, then very gentle mouth-to-mouth breathing at a slow rate may be started while being extremely careful to avoid rough handling of the victim.

If there are no signs of life, CPR and arrangements for emergency transport to the nearest medical facility should be started. Re-warming of the severely hypothermic victim cannot be accomplished in the field. CPR should be continued, if possible, until emergency assistance is obtained. There have been successful resuscitations after prolonged CPR, in part because of the protective effect of hypothermia.

Fig. 5.18 – *A survival suit can be quickly donned to rescue someone who has fallen through the ice*

Fig. 5.19 – *The tether helps the rescuer to exit the icy water*

Preventing chilling requires training, judgment and experience. The diver must understand the use of external insulation to conserve body heat and must be able to control heat loss. Recreational divers sometimes encounter very cold conditions in ice diving or winter diving in deep quarries and lakes. All ocean dives are in water below body temperature. Wet suits provide some degree of thermal protection depending on the style, material, and thickness, but they become compressed with increasing depth and lose much of their insulating properties. The "woolly bear" or open cell undergarment worn under a dry suit is effective, but also compresses and loses some insulation value. If wet, the "woolly bear" loses practically all of its insulating value. Type B marine Thinsulate® is an alternative which retains insulation value when wet.

The diver should be prepared for the actions to be taken once in the water. These include efforts to minimize heat loss, such as remaining still and assuming the H.E.L.P. position (heat escape lessening position). This position is assumed by drawing the knees up to the chest and holding with crossed arms. The position is unstable and not easy to achieve without practice, as one tends to roll forward or backward. Consequently, it is well to practice the position from time to time. The huddle position with other persons is surprisingly effective in conserving heat. Everyone wraps arms around one another and pulls into a tight circle, remaining as still as possible.

Conscious Diver with Lung Overpressure or DCI

Pulmonary barotrauma accidents can be a result of rapid ascent without exhalation. This can occur in ice diving situations where proper buoyancy is not maintained, because of freezing inflator mechanisms, or because of the loss of a weight belt. Signs and symptoms include difficulty breathing, pain in the chest, and in severe cases disturbed vision, unconsciousness, or paralysis.

Decompression illness can occur after dives supposedly within the "safe" limits of decompression tables or dive computers, or as the result of a rapid ascent. It is wise to plan dives in advance with adequate safety margins, to ascend slowly according to the specified rate for the tables or computer used, and to perform a precautionary stop for at least three minutes at a depth of 15 feet (5 m).

Fig. 5.20 – *If a diver tries to equalize pressure too vigorously, blood may appear in the mask. This is often more common in cold, dry climates.*

Fig. 5.21 – *Evacuation by helicopter may be required in remote locations (photo by Ken Dunton)*

Signs and symptoms include pain in the joints, skin rash, nausea, weakness, and in severe cases unconsciousness and paralysis.

The field first aid treatment for these situations is the same. The diver should be laid on his back and kept warm, CPR should be administered as needed, and 100% oxygen should be administered. Arrangements should be made for transportation to a medical facility and recompression chamber.

Unconscious Diver

An unconscious diver underwater is an extremely serious situation. Rescue procedures are similar to those for open water situations except for the presence of the tethers and overhead ice. The buddy should signal to the surface immediately with more than 4 pulls on the tether line. The diver should make contact with the unconscious diver, shake him, turn him to a face-up position if necessary, and establish a do-si-do position. If the regulator is in the victim's mouth, it should be left there. It may be necessary to release the weight belt of the victim to establish sufficient buoyancy for ascent. However, caution is advised here, as excessive positive buoyancy may be realized on ascent, causing potential danger to victim and rescuer alike. It is probably best to attempt ascent with the weight belt left in place. If the diver was neutrally buoyant or close to it at depth, then ascent should be relatively easy, and indeed air will have to be vented from each diver's suit on ascent. The safety diver may be able to assist with positioning the victim and venting air on ascent.

At the surface the tenders will assist in removing the diver from the water. Emergency help must be summoned immediately. The cylinder and weight belt must be removed from the diver, who is placed in a horizontal position on his back. A check for breathing must be made. Artificial respiration and CPR must be initiated if necessary. If the victim is in a hypothermic state, breathing and pulse rates may be very slow, so sufficient time and care should be given to checking for vital signs. The dry suit will have to be removed from the upper torso to perform CPR properly. Oxygen should be administered if required. The diver must also be sheltered from the cold, preferably in a heated shelter.

Depending upon the location of the dive site, and the nearest medical treatment facilities, a diver may have to be evacuated by helicopter. The importance of having a well thought out emergency plan cannot be over stressed in remote locations.

Summary

Ice diving is a potentially dangerous activity, therefore safety is of paramount importance. An emergency plan should be developed, reviewed, and practiced in simulation. It is important to recognize that rescue operations may be hampered by weather, cold, and remote locations. Prevention of accidents is the best policy to operate by.

References

Antarctic Scientific Diving Manual. 1994. Antarctic Support Associates (ASA), Englewood, Colorado. 128 pp.

Barsky, S.B. 1990. Diving in High Risk Environments. Dive Rescue Inc. International, Fort Collins, CO. 118 pp.

Barsky, S.B. and J.N. Heine. 1988. Observations of flooded dry suit buoyancy characteristics. In: Advances in Underwater Science '88: Proceedings of the American Academy of Underwater Sciences, M. Lang, (Ed.). American Academy of Underwater Sciences, Nahant, MA. p. 1-11.

Barsky, S.B., D. Long, and B. Stinton. 1992. Dry Suit Diving: A Guide to Diving Dry. Watersport Publ., Inc. San Diego, CA. 185 pp.

Bright, C.V. Diving in the Arctic. U.S. Naval Oceanographic Office. p. 1-12.

Cinnamon, J. 1994. Climbing Rock and Ice: Learning the Vertical Dance. Ragged Mountain Press, Camden, ME. 308 pp.

Flemming, N.C. and M.D. Max. 1988. Code for Practice of Scientific Diving: Principles for the safe practice of scientific diving in different environments. UNESCO, Paris, France. 251 pp.

Gloersen, P., Campbell, W.J., and D.J. Cavalleri et al. 1992. Arctic and Antarctic Sea Ice, 1978-1987: Satellite Passive-Microwave Observations and Analysis. National Aeronautics and Space Administration. 290 pp.

Heine, J.N. 1995. Advanced Diving: Technology and Techniques. Nat. Assoc. Underwater Instr. (NAUI). 293 pp.

Heine, J.N. 1995. Diving Dry: Skills and Techniques. Nat. Assoc. Underwater Instr. (NAUI). 37 pp.

Hendrick, B. The Parameters of Safe Ice Diving. In: SOURCES: The Journal of Underwater Education. National Association of Underwater Instructors, Montclair, CA. Mar. 1994. pgs. 37-40.

Jenkins, W.T. 1976. A Guide to Polar Diving. U.S. Navy. ONR Oceans Technology Programs Office Project RF-51-523-101. 89 pgs.

Lamb, I.M. and M.H. Zimmermann. 1977. Benthic Marine Algae of the Antarctic Peninsula. In: D.L. Pawson, Ed. Biology of the Antarctic Seas V , American Geophysical Union, Washington, D.C. pgs. 130-227.

Long, R. 1989. Dive suit buoyancy control problems and solutions. In: Proceedings of the Biomechanics of Safe Ascents Workshop. Egstrom, G. and M. Lang (Eds.). American Academy of Underwater Sciences, Nahant, MA. pgs. 103-110.

Madigan, D.L. 1984. Sunlight degradation of rope. National Safety News. p. 54-56.

Mastro, J. and N. Pollock. 1995. Regulator Testing Report, Scientific Diving Locker, McMurdo Station.

Mercer, S. 1992. Antarctic Diving Manual. New Zealand Antarctic Programme. 35 pp.

McMullen, J. 1992. The Basic Essentials of Climbing Ice. ICS Books, Inc. Merrillville, IN. 66 pp.

Neushul, M. 1961. Diving in Antarctic Waters. Polar Record vol. 10, no. 67, pp. 353-358.

Neushul, M. 1965. Diving Observations of Sub-Tidal Antarctic Marine Vegetation. Bot. Mar. vol. 8 pp. 234-243.

NOAA Diving Manual, Diving for Science and Technology. 1975, and 1991. U.S. Dept. of Commerce, NOAA.

Palmer, R. 1994. An Introduction to Technical Diving. Underwater World Publ., England. 119 pp.

Peckham, V. 1964. Year-round Scuba Diving in the Antarctic. Polar Record vol. 12, no. 77, pp. 143-146.

Rey, L. 1985. Arctic Underwater Operations. Proc. Intl. Conf. IceDive '84. London, Graham, and Trotman, Ltd. 356 pp.

Skreslet, S. and F. Aarefjord. 1968. Acclimatization to cold in man induced by frequent scuba diving in cold water. J. Appl. Physiol. 24, 177-181.

Somers, L.H. 1991. The Cold Water Diver's Handbook. University of Michigan, Ann Arbor, MI. 134 pp.

Standard First Aid. American Red Cross. 1993. 231 pp.

Stinton, R. 1989. Dry suit valves and performance. In: Proceedings of the Biomechanics of Safe Ascents Workshop. Egstrom, G. and M. Lang (Eds.). American Academy of Underwater Sciences, Nahant, MA. pgs. 111-122.

Index

Planning 83
Polar ice 15
Polypropylene 43, 61, 63, 64
Pressure ridges 73
Primary regulator 98

Q

Qualofil® 64

R

Radiant barrier 44
Regulator 19, 20, 23, 26, 52, 53-56, 57, 59, 60, 62, 84, 85, 86, 88, 97, 98, 103, 117
Regulator freeze-up 22
Research diving 3
Reverse stratification 7
Rivers 12, 14
Rope bag 87
Rubber 40

S

Safety 1, 3, 19, 22, 61, 77, 95-96, 105, 118
Safety diver 21, 23, 81, 87, 88, 100, 101, 103, 109, 118
Safety equipment 96
Safety harness 20, 61, 62, 98
Safety holes 81
Safety lines 19, 61, 62, 67, 73, 81, 100, 101
Safety stop 89, 92
Screw 104
Scuba 2, 4
Sea ice 76
Seals 24, 33, 35, 36, 37, 40, 41, 42, 48, 49, 51, 99, 102
Sediment 12, 13, 36, 86, 104

Shell suits 33, 36
Shelter 1, 19, 21, 25, 74, 77, 78, 89, 113
Shovel 21, 67, 77, 79, 82, 84
Siberia 10
Single hose scuba 53
Sled 67, 75, 79
Snow blindness 19, 105
Snow ice 13
Snowmobile 67, 73, 79, 84
Spokes 77, 84
Spring turnover 7
Standby diver 63, 101, 104
Stratification 5, 20
Stratified 8
Strobe flashers 104
Sunburn 19, 105
Sunglasses 65, 105
Surface supplied diving 60, 67
Survival suit 114

T

Tender 21, 24, 25, 27, 61, 65, 69, 70, 74, 78, 81, 83, 84, 85, 87, 89, 90, 93, 94, 96, 96, 101, 103, 104, 105, 118
Tender equipment 20
Tending 26, 64
Tethers 69, 87, 96, 103, 115, 117
Tether lines 20, 69, 78, 85, 87, 91, 101, 102, 103, 107, 117
Tethered 3, 86
Tethering 52
Thermoclines 5, 9, 10, 13
Thinsulate® 44, 47, 64, 115
Thintech® 64
Toboggan 67, 75